SS CANBERRA

SS CANBERRA

WILLIAM H MILLER

TEMPUS

for PETER KNEGO

his superb work in documenting passenger ships
has been remarkable – his dedication, discipline & energy
almost unequalled

First published 2007

Tempus Publishing Limited
The Mill, Brimscombe Port,
Stroud, Gloucestershire, GL5 2QG
www.tempus-publishing.com

© William H. Miller, 2007

British Library Cataloguing in Publication Data.
A catalogue record for this book is available from the British Library.

ISBN 978-0-7524-4211-2

Typesetting and origination by Tempus Publishing Limited
Printed in Great Britain

Cover illustration painted by Robert Lloyd.

CONTENTS

Foreword   6

Introduction   7

Acknowledgements   8

Foreword   7

1   P&O-Orient Liners: The Biggest Bloomin' Ships   9
     on all the Seas

2   Birth of a Legend   17

3   Three to 103 Days   25

4   Going Cruising   41

5   Heroic Days: Mission to the Falklands   60

6   Back in Business   65

7   End of a Grand Career   89

     Bibliography   96

FOREWORD

She was hailed as 'The Ship that Shapes the Future' and I first gazed at the beautiful lines of *Canberra* in the shimmering heat of Aden Harbor in June 1961. She was on her maiden voyage to Australia and I was an eight year old who was fascinated by ships. The harbor in those days was always full of interest and one could spend hours watching the many wonderful ships of that era.

Canberra was moored to buoys a short distance off Prince of Wales Pier and was helped in her maneuver by the tug *Champion*. She only spent a few hours in port to take on bunkers, but I was to see her on subsequent calls as she sped between England and Australasia and the Pacific. The P&O building at Steamer Point was most modern and impressive, and it was here that a few months later passes were obtained to visit *Canberra*. I could not have wished for anything more than to step on board the cutting-edge world that the ship represented. My father recorded the event on beautiful Kodachrome slides, which I still look at today if I want to be taken back to another time.

When I think of *Canberra*, I always think of those days. A fast, powerful ocean liner with wonderful first class accommodations and stunning design features. The grace of her twin, streamlined funnels have never been equaled, for example. Of course, she was not without her critics. Many felt that due to her speed, size, air-conditioning and glass windbreaks on the top deck, that one was remote from the sea when traveling on board. It was not like the adventure of, say, being on a plodding smaller ship with breezy open decks, and so her consort in the days of P&O-Orient Lines, the slightly smaller *Oriana*, was favored by many too. However, as a ship that remained with one company and externally looking the same for her entire career, *Canberra*

outlived them all. Even her propulsion system remained original. In later years with even *Oriana* gone, she became one of the most popular ships in the much changed world of one-class cruising.

After I left school, I joined P&O as a deck cadet and served in all ranks on *Canberra* up to Deputy Captain. While still a relative youngster, I remember being appointed Senior Second Officer – the Navigator – and being called for my first watch in that capacity at 4:00 a.m. as we sped southwest in the English Channel and the feeling of intense pride for my new responsibilities.

I last saw *Canberra* as I drove away from Southampton Docks as she departed for the breakers' beach in Pakistan. I had wonderful memories of the ship and so I hope you will enjoy this history written so expertly by Bill Miller as there are few ships that have been through so much. She was fascinating from her maiden voyage onward and remains so today. But as you will read, it was not always smooth sailing for *Canberra* and that was the case that afternoon as we waited on the Aden waterfront to watch her depart on her maiden call. Her passengers returned from their shopping spree, the sun had set and the harbor grew dark, but then her lights did not come on. Power was restored later that night and she departed in the early hours. Advanced design brings its problems and that was *Canberra* – a wonderful ship!

Captain Nick Carlton
Master, *Grand Princess*
October 2006

INTRODUCTION

Several times a year, but more often during summer school holidays, I would travel over by ferryboat to Lower Manhattan, specifically to 'Shipping Row' along the very bottom of Broadway. My destination: the great and then plentiful shipping offices. There was Holland America, the Italian Line, Furness Bermuda, Norwegian America and many others, but the greatest and grandest of them of all was by far the splendid lower-floor reception and then magnificent rotunda of the Cunard Steam-Ship Company Limited as it was called. Amidst the rows of mahogany desks, the superbly worked, gilded and mosaic three-storey-high ceiling, and one of the finest collections of detailed marine models anywhere, there was a display rack off to the left side of the Great Hall that offered printed matter – those brochures, deck plans, rate sheets and sailing schedules – of passenger ship companies, all of them British or British-connected, that sailed on worldwide routes but away from New York. By the late 1950s, as I remember, P&O-Orient Lines had the greatest collection, the biggest liner fleet (apart from Cunard itself and its dozen liners) and the most far-flung, diverse schedules. P&O-Orient passenger services were linked to Cunard and their Atlantic crossings, and such that, at a 25 Broadway booking agent's well-polished desk (complete with green-domed lamp and bulky Bakelite phone), a prospective voyager could book, say, the *Queen Mary* to Southampton and connect with, say, the *Himalaya* at London-Tilbury, and sail to Sydney via the Mediterranean, Suez and the Indian Ocean. You could then stay in Australia for a time, for example, and then connect homeward to the US, to Los Angeles or San Francisco, on a Pacific voyage of, say, the *Arcadia*. A voyage of a total of some eight weeks on three different ships was thus arranged in, perhaps, an hour's session at 25

Broadway. I visited those offices for a different reason, however – to collect the latest brochures. Especially, I recall the first, preliminary fold-out on the two 'super liners' that were then still under construction: the *Oriana* for the Orient Line and due in late 1960 and, bigger still, the *Canberra* for P&O and scheduled for commissioning in mid-1961. Such excitement, such new ships, such advanced design!

Living in Hoboken, the New Jersey waterfront city just across the Hudson River from New York City, I waited patiently along the banks on a flawless summer afternoon in 1962. Normal shipping continued, other liners and freighters came and went, and the ever-plentiful smaller harborcraft sailed about, but there was a very special visitor that day: the *Canberra* was arriving for the first time. Dressed in flags and escorted by Moran tugs and other vessels, she came into my view rather slowly, indeed majestically, heading upriver and appearing from behind the shed of Hoboken's old Ninth Street pier. Beautiful, sleek and extraordinarily modern, almost futuristic, she was, I felt, one of the finest-looking new liners I had yet seen. She was indeed a great beauty! A day or so later I watched her, but from a different Jersey vantage point, as she sat at Cunard's Pier 90, seemingly surrounded by other well-known New York liners, ships such as the *Independence, Queen Frederica, Italia, Queen of Bermuda* and *Ocean Monarch*. The all-white *Canberra* towered over all of them, however, and noticeably compared in her lines and very contemporary design with the likes of, say, the veteran, thirty-four-year-old *Italia*.

Almost eleven years passed until, in January 1973, I had my first visit to the mighty P&O flagship and then a further seven years, in October 1980, before I sailed on her for the first time. Three voyages followed. She has been, of course, included in many of my previous books, in photographs and in documenting her distinguished career. Of course, with great sorrow, I noted her retirement in the fall of 1997 and then her sale to Mid-Eastern scrappers. Her thirty-six-year record was exceptional – some 1,000,000 passengers carried and about 3,000,000 miles steamed – and surpassed, in modern memory, only by another great British liner, Cunard's *Queen Elizabeth 2*. The *Canberra* is indeed special is many ways.

It is therefore with great pleasure and high interest that I pen this review of the beautiful *Canberra,* one of the most popular and beloved and, assuredly, successful liners of all time.

Bill Miller
Secaucus, New Jersey, USA
Summer 2006

ACKNOWLEDGEMENTS

Compiling a book such as *SS Canberra* takes a 'full crew'. I am merely the cruise director of sorts, organizing words, anecdotes, comments and photographs. So, I would like to offer my warmest thanks to Campbell McCutcheon and his fine staff at Tempus for suggesting and then creating this tribute to our beloved P&O flagship. Special thanks to the superb Robert Lloyd for his specially created artworks and to my friend Captain nick Carlton of P&O, who graciously offered some introductory words. Added first-class thanks to two splendid photographers, Peter Knego and Fred Rodriguez, who generously shared of their massive collections.

Further appreciation is due to Bob Allen, the late Frank Andrews, Barry Banyard, Scott Batty, Frank Braynard, the late Ted Birkett, Stephen Card, Tom Cassidy, Tom Chirby, Dr Peter Crimes, Luis Miguel Correia, Richard Faber, Ginger Fortin, Howard Franklin, Joann Hastings, Clive Harvey, Alan Hatcher, Brad Hatry, Stanley Haviland, the late Doreen Heywood, Charles Howland, David Hutchings, the late Frank Jackson, Marvin Jensen, Dr Rick Jolly, Des Kirkpatrick, the late Dean Miller, the late Stanley Miller, Robert Pelletier, Tony Ralph, Captain Martin Reed, Linette Reynolds, Der Scutt, Captain Ed Squire, Frank Trumbour, Ken Vard and Jeffrey Willis.

Firms and organizations due thanks include Crystal Cruises, Cunard Line, the Ocean Liner Council at the South Street Seaport, P&O, Port Authority of New York and New Jersey, the Port Everglades Authority, Steamship Historical Society of America (especially the long Island, New York branch), Saga Cruises, Southern Newspapers Ltd and World Ship Society (especially the Port of New York branch).

P&O-ORIENT LINERS: THE BIGGEST BLOOMIN' SHIPS ON ALL THE SEAS

I had not seen a P&O-Orient liner until I was eleven, in 1959, as both the *Arcadia* and *Iberia* made calls at New York as part of three-week cruises from Southampton and that included three-day, two-night 'hotel stays' along Manhattan's West Side. I was impressed with the beauty of these liners, but also rather amazed by their size. They were equal to many transatlantic liners, ships such as the *Nieuw Amsterdam*, *America* and *Caronia*, in height, length and sheer might. I watched as both the *Arcadia* and *Iberia* made early evening departures, slipping past the city skyline and making their way along the Hudson River. Using Laurence Dunn's *British Passenger Liners* (published in 1959) as my reference point, it seemed a rather unusual year for a young ocean liner enthusiast such as myself. That summer, the *Andes* of Royal Mail Lines called at New York as well. So, in all, there were three unusual British liners paying visits and, thereafter, my interest in P&O-Orient in particular was heightened.

P&O-Orient Line passenger ships were legendary in many ways. They were also very evocative, especially to the likes of Americans. P&O lecturer and marine author Ken Vard noted, 'The P&O-Orient passenger ships of the post-war period were the last of the classic, British blue water liners. They were created for two classes of passengers, originally for the Indian and Australian service before India became independent in 1947. Later, the tourist class was filled with ten-pound poms (emigrants on assisted passages to Australia) and first class with elegant, wealthy passengers from both sides of the equator.'

'My personal memory of some of the ships was as a passenger cruising from the UK and especially onboard the *Arcadia* for my first cruise with my parents when the ship was only four months in service [1954],' added Vard. 'I remember her with great affection as a glamorous, huge, all-white liner, oozing a smell of polish, cigars, expensive perfume and a hint of curry. We were in first class and I had my first white tuxedo for the many formal nights. We did not have private toilets or baths then – to bathe meant booking with the steward for a hot saltwater or fresh-water bath. He would supply the large, warmed towels and bring you to the private room down the corridor. The doors to the cabins were louvered for extra ventilation since there was no air-conditioning, except in the restaurant, back then. I remember having the porthole open and hearing the sea rushing by and smelling the salt air at night. It was wonderful!'

'In the mornings, I watched the Lascar crew on their knees holy-stoning the teak decks under the eye of a Serang [head man] dressed in blue tunic and red turban,' he added. 'Stewards in first class were European and those in tourist were Goanese from India. I thought it was all so exotic. And I had my first curry aboard the *Arcadia*. P&O curries are still a feature onboard even today, although not as authentic as in the old days. The public rooms were elegant and lined with rare woods, the corridors were covered with lino and only the lounge and library were carpeted as I recall. Dancing, cinema shows, horse racing and bingo were all held in a room with screens that could be lifted to the deck head and so creating a space the full width of the ship open to the air. We would sit on cane chairs watching a movie with the breezes blowing around us. It was quite magical! It all had the feeling of luxury combined with adventure, both somehow lacking in today's wonder ships. Exclusivity seemed to pervade the passengers, at least in first class, but tourist class was actually not much different, even if smaller in area. Each class had open decks and a swimming pool with terrace. The cruise on the *Arcadia* was to the Med and we called at four ports, overnighting in each. It was all great fun, especially for us younger passengers, who went along with junior officers and cadets to nightclubs ashore and then coming back to the ship after midnight to get a full breakfast including fresh bread from the ovens before going to bed. The Bay of Biscay was rough, as I remember, and there were no anti-seasick pills then. But I was fed Rum & Coke as a cure. But I cannot remember if I was sick or not!'

By 1960, as P&O and the Orient Line were officially coupled, their passenger ship fleet seemed immense: sixteen liners in all. P&O had the *Arcadia* and *Iberia* (29,000 tons), the *Himalaya* (28,000 tons), *Chusan* (24,000 tons), the *Stratheden* (23,000 tons), the *Strathmore* (23,000 tons), the sisters *Strathaird* and *Strathnaver* (22,000 tons), the *Canton* (16,000 tons) and, also sisters, the *Carthage* and the *Corfu* (14,000 tons). Orient Line had the *Orsova* (28,000 tons), *Oronsay* (27,000 tons), *Orcades* (28,000 tons), *Orion* (23,000 tons) and *Orontes* (20,000 tons). Routes were primarily from Europe to Australia, either via the Suez or Panama Canal routes, but also to the Far East and including North American ports. In all, voyages ranged from two to 102 days, touching upon over 100 ports of call.

Primarily interested in the booming UK-Australia run, however, Company directors were, beginning in the mid-1950s, looking for new passenger routes. In 1954, they reached across the Pacific, northward from Australia to the North American West Coast – to Vancouver, San Francisco and Los Angeles. Four years later, in 1958, the *Himalaya* made the first of regular voyages from Australia and New Zealand to North America. P&O-Orient just about covered the world. The Pacific, in particular, was seen to be the 'last frontier' of ocean travel and, as support, prompted the construction of two, large, very fast, high-capacity 'super liners'.

Historically, when the 1,416-passenger *Oronsay* reached Sydney in the spring of 1954, she did not return to London via the Suez Canal as would have been the custom, but instead went northwards in the Pacific to Los Angeles, San Francisco and Vancouver. This was the beginning of what would become known in North America as the Orient & Pacific Line, the forerunner to P&O-Orient Lines and later to Princess Cruises, P&O's North American cruising subsidiary.

Gradually, the infant Orient & Pacific Line took hold in the minds of North American travel agents and the traveling public itself. There were these big, brightly painted, two-class ocean liners with names like *Arcadia, Chusan, Orsova* and *Orcades*. First class tended to British tropical – with lots of rattan furniture mixed with floral print sofas and chairs; tourist class was almost austere, indeed very basic and unabashedly had the likes of exposed piping and wiring along the public ceilings. But for as little as $10 per person per day in a tourist class minimum room, business grew.

'By 1954, there was a great void in Pacific ocean travel,' according to the late Dean Miller, P&O-Orient's public relations representative in Vancouver for over thirty years. 'The pre-war Canadian Pacific liner service to the Far East was never resumed and Union Line's *Aorangi*, which ran from Australia and New Zealand to Vancouver, had just been retired and was not replaced. So, the Orient Line decided to experiment by going from Australia to the North American West Coast. The first trip was made by the *Oronsay* and then two trips followed on the old *Orion*, dating from 1935. The initial response was encouraging, especially because of lingering Second World War connections, and in particular marriages. Many American GI's had gone out to Australia and married local girls, and then there were Australian and New Zealand servicemen who had come up to Canada for air training programs and married Canadian girls. Consequently, by the mid-1950s, when there were children and even some grandchildren, and in the buoyant age of post-war prosperity, there was a need for sea voyage connections. This was Orient Line's success and meant twelve voyages to the West Coast within three years, by 1957.'

'While they were keen competitors on the UK-Australia route, Orient Line's success led to discussions with the P&O Lines to expand as well,' added Miller. 'Let's make the Pacific a British ocean' was the theme. So, the Orient Line's *Orcades, Oronsay* and *Orsova* were soon joined by the *Himalaya, Chusan, Arcadia* and *Iberia*. And their success would support the construction of two, far larger liners, the *Canberra* and *Oriana*. P&O's appearance also meant that the service to North America could be expanded to include the Far East as well, from ports such as Singapore, Hong Kong, Kobe and Yokohama. The *Chusan* made the first Far East passage to Vancouver and, by early 1958, it had all fallen into place with the *Himalaya*'s inaugural trip from Auckland and Wellington to Vancouver.'

Above left: Canberra was and remains one of the most important, popular and beloved ships in the British merchant navy. (Fred Rodriguez Collection)

Above middle: The roots of the great and historic P&O Company are in voyages out East, on sailings beyond Suez and in particular to India and Australia. Sailings from ports such as Sydney were often very festive, even emotional events. (Author's Collection)

Above right: P&O and the Orient Line are fondly remembered in many ports of the world, but especially in Australia. Here we see another gala departure from Sydney, in a view dated 1939, aboard the *Orcades*. (Author's Collection)

In P&O-Orient's post-Second World War fleet, a number of pre-war liners remained including the 20,100-ton *Orontes*, dating from 1929 and shown here, and the 23,600-ton *Orion* of 1935. (Author's Collection)

Many responded to P&O and Orient Line's enthusiastic advertising in the 1950s and '60s and made voyages not only to Australia, but to ports around the world. (Author's Collection)

There were also the four famous 'Strath liners' — the *Strathnaver* and *Strathaird* of 1931-32, the *Strathmore* of 1935 and the *Stratheden* from 1937 (shown here during a rare visit to New York in 1950). (Author's Collection)

The 28,300-ton *Orcades* was the first of Orient Line's post-war newbuilds. Built at Vickers at Barrow, she was commissioned in December 1948, carrying 631 in first class and 734 in tourist. (Author's Collection)

The 27,900-ton *Himalaya*, seen here at Sydney in 1972, was P&O's first post-war addition. She had her maiden voyage in December 1949. (Frank Andrews Collection)

The 24,200-ton *Chusan* joined P&O in June 1950, but rather than for the UK-Australian trade, she sailed primarily on the UK-Far East run. She is shown here at Southampton in 1964. (Author's Collection)

10 The 27,600-ton *Oronsay* was a refined version of the earlier *Orcades* and she joined the Orient Line schedules in May 1951. Seen here at Sydney, she could carry 612 passengers in first class and 804 in tourist. (Author's Collection)

Above left: The *Arcadia* and her near-sister *Iberia* were the 'rave sensations' for P&O in 1954. Seen here departing from Sydney in February 1972, the 29,700-ton *Arcadia* was launched on 14 May 1953, coincidentally the same day as Orient Line's new flagship *Orsova*. (Frank Andrews Collection)

Above right The Belfast-built, 721ft-long *Iberia* joined P&O in September 1954. She is seen here, however, on her final sailing from Sydney in February 1972. She would soon be retired and sold to Taiwanese scrap merchants, the beginning of a 'parade to the block' for much of the post-war P&O-Orient Lines' fleet. (Frank Andrews Collection)

Left: The 28,700-ton *Orsova*, which joined the Orient Line in May 1954, was quite novel in being the first large liner to dispense with the conventional mast. (Author's Collection)

Above: Twin sisters, the 13,900-ton *Chitral* (shown here at Sydney in 1972) and *Cathay*, were bought from the Belgian Line in 1961 for the UK-Far East run. Much like 'big yachts', they were combination passenger-cargo liners that carried only 240 all-first class passengers. (Frank Andrews Collection)

Above right: The 41,923-ton *Oriana* (shown at Sydney's Circular Quay in June 1984) was the first of the two new 'big liners' built for P&O-Orient's Australian as well as expanding round-the-world services. Commissioned in December 1960, she cut the passage time between Southampton and Sydney via Suez by one week, to twenty-one days. (Author's Collection)

Built by Vickers-Armstrong at Barrow, the 804ft-long *Oriana* was unique in having two funnels but at different levels. The aft one was a dummy-ventilator, but the effect gave her a rather curious, almost eccentric, but certainly distinctive look. (Author's Collection)

The *Oriana*'s interiors were modern in style. (Author's Collection)

Many of her public areas were styled for long periods of sea travel, those often cherished days at sea. (Author's Collection)

2

BIRTH OF A LEGEND

'She said more about the shpe of ships to come than probably any other new liner,' recalled Tony Ralph, who was watching as a young student along the dockside at Sydney when the new P&O Line's flagship arrived there for the first time. It was the summer of 1961 and the 44,000-tonner, then the largest passenger ship built for a service other than the prestigious, very competitive North Atlantic trade, was news, very big news in fact. She made headlines and was the subject of countless newspaper and magazine supplements. She was big (818ft in length), fast (27 knots and more) and wonderfully modern (very comfortable, fully air-conditioned, two-class quarters for some 2,200 travelers). And she looked futuristic with her twin uptakes (instead of traditional smokestacks) placed aft, her swimming pools amidships and her lifeboats being tucked away on lower decks rather than up high. Her bow was raked, her foredecks rounded and her bridge and wheelhouse areas mounted in almost turret style.

'She showed us the future,' added Tony Ralph, today a keen ship enthusiast, ocean liner historian and shore excursion manager at Cunard. 'She had a very clean design that was light years away from the previous liners on the Australian trade. The lifeboats being stowed on a lower deck had only been seen once before, on the Dutch *Willem Ruys*. The funnels were unique and her modern interiors, including a circular staircase, were quite exceptional design features at the time. And the pools and lido areas being placed in the mid-ships section was also eye-catching. Some outer decks were arranged stadium-style, which was a big change from those long rows of deckchairs of the past.'

P&O Captain Nick Carlton recalled her as well from those inaugural days of the early '60s. 'She was the Concorde of her time,' he said when in command, years later, of the Bermuda-bound *Pacific Princess*. 'She was the future. And she was a great sight, anywhere and from any angle.'

The *Canberra* had many distinctions. Among them, she was the very last 'ocean liner' built for P&O and the last liner created by Harland & Wolff. There were other, perhaps lesser, details. Architect Der Scutt reminded us of some. 'Because of her unique lifeboat configuration, new gravity davits were designed to launch 17-ton, fully-laden lifeboats against a 25-degree adverse list with a 10-degree trim. This was quite advanced in 1961. Of further interest, it should be noted that the Scottish Machine Tool Corporation had just developed a method for strengthening exterior roll plating using larger-capacity frame benders; the frames were beveled in a cold process which led to a longer life of the ship and greater safety. There was also the innovative Collis conveying systems for both on- and off-loading and which did not deter from clean exterior lines of the ship itself. A new and advanced solvent-less epoxide coating was created, which had the equivalent to 4-5 tons of paint. This contributed to the continued visual enhancement of the ship without frequent repainting traditionally common to other ships. These details aside, the *Canberra* was a magnificent ocean liner, whose image was different and distinctive from all other liners in existence at the time. Her exterior profile and styling has contributed much to current design philosophies of today's cruise ships.'

Soon after the commissioning of the 29,000-ton, 1,500-passenger near-sisters *Arcadia* and *Iberia* in 1954, P&O directors had asked managers and their designers to begin making very general plans for a far larger, faster, even innovative liner. She might be as large as 35,000 tons, so the first notes suggested. By 1956, P&O requested all major British shipyards to submit bids for the construction of this new, larger liner. Rumors were at this point that she would weigh over 40,000 tons and clearly be the biggest P&O ship ever. John Brown on the Clyde, Vickers-Armstrong at Barrow-in-Furness and Swan, Hunter & Wigham Richardson at Newcastle were among those interested. But it was the builders of the handsome-looking *Iberia* that received the most attention and finally the secure order. Five days before Christmas 1956, P&O's London office announced that Harland & Wolff of Belfast in Northern Ireland had the job. Creators of the likes of the *Titanic*, *Olympic* and that third giant White Star liner, the *Britannic*, the Company had an otherwise very fine reputation. More recently, in the late 1940s, they built the 28,000-ton sisters *Edinburgh Castle* and *Pretoria Castle*, the largest Union-Castle liners to date. By 1955, they had completed the 20,000-ton *Southern Cross* for Shaw Savill Line, the first major liner to have her engines and therefore funnel mounted aft. She might just have been the most innovative liner of the mid-1950s and certainly spelled the way for the future of passenger ship design. A huge success, the *Southern Cross* caught the eye of many other passenger ship companies, including P&O directors, and much inspired their original concepts for their new liner. So she too, it was decided, would have her engines and funnels aft.

Soon after the building order was signed, in January 1956, P&O announced firmer, alluring details of their new super ship – about 45,000 tons, 818ft in length and 103ft wide. The public was already intrigued. And, it was rumored, she would have the great speed to sail, say, between Southampton and Sydney in little more than three weeks, using as much as 85,000 horsepower. She was known only as '1621,' her yard number.

As the months passed, other details were tantalizingly revealed. With her funnels and engines being aft, it was reported that the better part of the ship would therefore be given over to passenger quarters. Unusual for the time, her lifeboats would sit in retractable davits that would recess into a lower deck of the superstructure as opposed to being topside, on the Boat Deck. Also, a great deal of aluminium would be used in the superstructure, saving about 1,500 tons in total weight and allowing the designers to create and fit an additional 200 cabins.

The first keel plates were laid on an autumn morning, 23 September 1957, in Slipway 14 of Harland & Wolff's Queens Island yard at Belfast. Six months later, the name *Canberra* – meaning 'meeting place' in Maori and, of course, the capital city of Australia – was announced. There had been a small Australian passenger ship of the same name and which sailed as the *Canberra* until 1954 and later also a warship named *Canberra*. As time passed, interest mounted for the new P&O liner. A large model of her was put on display at the 1958 World's Fair in Brussels and during the Olympic Games in 1960 and at the Queensland Centenary Exhibition.

Maritime author and historian David Hutchings was one of the young boys who lived in and around Southampton who was caught up in the mounting excitement for the big, new P&O flagship. 'My first contact with the *Canberra* came through a children television series called *Crow's Nest*. This was broadcast in the late 1950s and, in a series of six programs, John West, the young designer of the liner, gave a weekly progress report on the building of the ship and demonstrated how a scale model of the liner could be built. Plans for the model could be sent (for), but my copy has disappeared over the years. In the final program, I seem to remember that the model was "launched".'

'At the end of each week's show, John West would draw, on a blackboard and using old-fashioned chalk, the funnel and mast arrangement of a 'mystery ship' [the *Canberra*]. The young viewers were then invited to identify the ship represented, draw the whole vessel on a postcard and submit their efforts for a prize. I dutifully entered the competition each week until my name was read out one day as one of the lucky prize-winning entrants. However, my prize did not materialize, but a subsequent letter to the producer brought forth a book voucher for 17s 6d (or 85p in 'modern money') with which I bought Laurence Dunn's excellent little book on the Cunard Line, which was a real treasure in those days as not many such books were available.'

'Another remembered and eagerly anticipated event was the appearance of a cutaway of the *Canberra* in the boys' classic comic *Eagle* with its weekly series depicting the adventures of those such as Dan Dare – Pilot of the Future, Luck of the Legion, Riders of the Range and so on. It was all great stuff! These double-paged center spread, color cutaways were usually drawn by Laurence Dunn, a chap named Fisher or other artists. Other engineering achievements other than ships also made appearances, but they seemed less important to me.'

What a gloriously proud day for the illustrious Harland & Wolff yard at Belfast. On 16 March 1960, the gleaming hull of the mighty *Canberra* was launched. Thousands were present as Dame Pattie Menzies, wife of the then Australian Prime Minister, named the charismatic, record-breaking liner. Unfortunately, it was a cold, wet day. A flypast by a Canberra bomber had to be canceled, for example, flags and banners hung limp and gray skies hovered overhead. But 300 invited guests were invited to the launch while another 11,000 onlookers crammed around the towering white hull. She was the largest liner of any flag to be built for a service other than the North Atlantic and the biggest, longest and tallest British liner since the *Queen Elizabeth* in the late 1930s. P&O-Orient were proud – she was in every way a symbol of their great success, a hallmark of their rich and exceptional history and a strong testament to the future of not only the Australian liner trade, but to worldwide ocean liner travel in general. These were, in fact, boom times to British shipowners and, in particular, to British liner companies. Union Castle Line was adding not one, but two large liners, the *Windsor Castle* in 1960 and the *Transvaal Castle* a year or so later; Canadian Pacific was building their *Empress of Canada*; and Shaw Savill had their *Northern Star* on the ways. Of course, reverses, major changes in fact, arrived and then crashed down upon British shipping as well as shipbuilding in just a matter of years. Harland & Wolff would never again build a liner and P&O-Orient would never again create a traditional, class-divided liner. Worse still, Union Castle, Canadian Pacific and Shaw Savill would never again order a new passenger ship.

But the triumph and pride at the launch of the *Canberra* on that day in March 1960 was unbridled. She was the very best of British design, construction and technology. British newspapers, magazines and especially marine journals found her to be fascinating news. The interested public were, for example, intrigued and even preliminary reservations for her maiden voyage and other early sailings were coming in at P&O-Orient's offices in London.

When first planning for the innovative *Canberra* in 1954-55, the designs for the most recent P&O liners, the *Arcadia* and *Iberia,* were largely put aside. The new liner, far larger and faster and more comfortable to as many as 2,200 passengers, had to be innovative, different, far-reaching. She would be, after all, the 'Ship of the Future'. Orient Line, simultaneously designing their new liner, the *Oriana,* were innovative and forward-looking as well, but used the 29,000-ton, 1954-built *Orsova* as something of a role model. P&O opted to break new ground with the *Canberra*.

After launching, the *Canberra* was carefully towed to Harland & Wolff's Thompson Wharf for fitting-out, a task that lasted another thirteen months, until April 1961. She left on 29 April for her first trials, in Belfast Lough, but with a most embarrassing problem. At full speed, the weight in the stern section caused the bow to almost lift completely out of the water. The ship's machinery had created immense weight, far more than was calculated, in the aft section of the otherwise freshly painted, all-white liner. She was 500 tons overweight in the stern. Soon afterward, she was sent to Southampton, where some of her forward holds and compartments were filled with tons of cement that acted as a counterweight. This would be a problem, in fact a big problem, for the rest of her days. Harland & Wolff was embarrassed, P&O disturbed and it was hopefully the ship's first and only blemish.

She spent two weeks at Southampton, being further fitted-out and as 300 Harland & Wolff laborers and subcontractors worked around the clock to add the finishing touches to her interiors. Later, she went off to the Clyde for her final and formal trials, which, off the Isle of Arran, showed a top speed of 29.27 knots. Happily, P&O took formal delivery of their new flagship and then sent her to the southern coast of England to 'show off' a bit. She was seen off Lands End, at Torbay and as far east as Dover. She returned to Southampton and began use of a new passenger terminal built especially for her and the *Oriana*, which had been in service almost six months.

When she was commissioned in June 1961, the *Canberra* made front-page news. She was, after all, the biggest British liner to come along in over twenty years. The *Canberra* was also the largest P&O liner yet, the greatest and perhaps grandest ever for the England-Australia trade and a modern two-class ship with one of the highest peacetime capacities to put to sea in years, over 2,200 in all. In later life, she made the transition into a popular, all one-class cruise ship, did heroic service during Britain's Falklands War of 1982 and finally finished her thirty-six-year-long career as the beloved 'Great White Whale'. Indeed, she was one of Britain's finest liners. In all, there were five new British liners coming into service at just about the same time – namely, the *Pendennis Castle, Windsor Castle, Oriana, Empress of Canada* and *Northern Star*. But the *Canberra* was by far the most newsworthy. Alone, she had a very modern, very advanced exterior. Internally, she was most contemporary in every way, in fact a great contrast to earlier P&O-Orient liners, including the most recent, the *Arcadia, Iberia* and *Orsova* of 1954-55. The *Canberra* hinted of more, perhaps greater British liners to follow. But, in fact, a long sleep followed, one that was not broken until the maiden arrival of Cunard's 66,000-ton *Queen Elizabeth 2* in 1969.

'For ship lovers, the *Canberra* certainly occupies an important place in post-war linerdom,' according to Charles Howland, a New York-based enthusiast and collector. 'Her unique appearance certainly made her memorable. I remember seeing her on a rare visit to New York late in her career, and love her or not, her lines were unforgettable. Her place in liner history was by then already assured by her heroic service in the Falklands War.'

There was an almost instant comparison between the *Canberra* and the slightly smaller, but faster *Oriana*. 'The *Canberra* was a very different ship from the *Oriana*,' said Howland. 'She was not quite as fast, but some would say a far better interior layout. Ship lovers especially develop favorites and for all kinds of reasons, and I have to admit being partial to the *Oriana*. I felt she was the more distinctive looking of the two with a better balanced profile and a superior stance in the water.'

The great divide in opinion between the *Canberra* and *Oriana* was at its peak especially after the *Canberra* entered service in June 1961. 'I feel that the *Canberra* (along with the *Oriana*) held a unique spot in post-Second World War ocean liner history,' according to Robert Allen, an architect and world class ocean liner collector and sea traveler. 'She was at the same time a cutting-edge, ultra-modern vessel and yet a throwback to an earlier age. With her engines-aft design, turbo-electric propulsion, aluminum superstructure, acres of uncluttered, protected yet open deck spaces, nested lifeboats, glass enclosed observation lounges, "courtyard" cabin arrangements, crisp modern furniture and décor, and other innovations, she was one of the most revolutionary ships of the era. At the same time, her hundreds of cabins lacking private facilities, strict class divisions, window-less dining rooms and high fuel consumption made her virtually obsolete on her maiden voyage. To me, these two opposite ships built into the same hull will be one of her lasting legacies.'

'With exception of the engines-aft design, I've always felt that the *Canberra* and *Oriana* were quite similar; the innovations and weaknesses listed above applied to both,' added Allen. 'I do feel that the *Oriana* was undeservedly less admired than the *Canberra* because of her more traditional profile. Yet although *Oriana*'s profile was more traditional, it was revolutionary in its own way: funnels of different sizes set on different decks; an unusual massing of open and enclosed spaces; an overall shape more like a pyramid than a standard liner profile; unique shape and positioning of masts and cranes all added up to a stunning, refreshing new look as exciting to me as *Canberra* was. In my opinion, the layout and overall design of the *Oriana* was equal quality to that of the *Canberra*.'

Allen concluded on the subject of exterior design, 'The exterior of the *Canberra* strikes me as one of the cleanest, most simple and sleek of any funnels-aft liner ever built. The nested boats with the corresponding fenestration of the Arena Deck above was enormously successful as was the massing of the officers' accommodation and bridge with its uniquely sloped bulkhead/structural web aft. The sleek kingposts forward, rounded superstructure front, massive forward mast and well proportioned twin-boom funnels balanced the entire profile to perfection. While she was no doubt a great beauty among post-war liners, the Italian-built *Oceanic* is to my eye still the most stunning of the funnel-aft ships ever built.'

'The *Canberra* presented a dignified appearance with her graceful bow, and distinctive curving bridge front,' he concluded. 'I always felt her paired funnels weren't quite majestic enough, and were mounted just a little too far aft. Variations on her open sports decks and protected pool areas are seen on many contemporary cruise ships. In this way, she certainly was ahead of her time and assuredly a trend-setter. As with any prototype design, refinements would come with later ships, but the *Canberra* was not followed by any P&O variations on a theme until many years later.'

Stanley Haviland, a Sydney-based ocean liner collector and avid cruise traveler, recalled seeing the P&O flagship in the 1960s and '70s at that Australian port. 'Her exterior was the shape that made young boys like me want to design ships. Like many, I had the Airfix plastic model of her. Even when stationary, she always looked like she was moving. Her bridge front and her beautifully terraced and rounded stern were distinct features. But *Oriana* will always be my favorite of the two even though I never traveled on her. She was a lady from the beginning and was always more plush with her interiors. She wasn't as streamlined as the *Canberra*. But she had that wonderful knuckle line half-way down the bow, as did *Canberra*, and that ran back almost to the Stadium Deck on both. This gave them both a distinct hull shape even if the *Oriana* had much fuller stern and with her wonderful galleries overlooking the wake.'

'The *Canberra* was, arguably, the most important post-Second World War liner of those not designed to operate primarily on the North Atlantic,' commented New York-based ocean liner expert Brad Hatry. 'She was the last big ship designed for the England-Australia migrant trade. Her later conversion to a highly successful cruise ship after several 'near death' experiences was quite notable and then there was her heroic Falklands service. She had continued popularity right until the end.'

Bournemouth-based ocean liner collector Alan Hatcher added, 'The *Canberra* was of ground-breaking design, following in the footsteps of the *Rotterdam* of 1959, with her funnels moved aft instead of the then more traditional amidships. This design was to influence the shape of ships to come and we can see some forty-five years later that way of thinking is still very much evident. And she was a ship of great personality and position. She had a large and loyal following, was famous in that she did war duty in the Falklands and overall gave sterling service to P&O. And she was a pioneer of sorts in cruising. I would place her second only to the *QE2*.'

'I found her exterior extremely easy to digest as with *Oriana*,' added Hatcher, 'but in the end I would choose *Canberra*.'

Comparison's to Orient Line's *Oriana* was especially common when the two big liners were first completed in the early '60s. 'Of the two, the *Canberra* was the more externally attractive, probably amongst the best looking of all post-war liners. The *Oriana* was quirky on the outside, to say the least. She was not unattractive, however. One of *Canberra*'s greatest strengths was her lovely exterior profile and superb outer decks. Few liners of any era can compare. From the knuckled bow forward to the gracefully curved funnels aft, and with the beautiful sheer and nestled lifeboats in between, she had few peers. Her outer decks were absolutely superb. The first class Bonito Pool, surrounded by those lovely terraced decks, was the perfect place to stop for a swim and cool drink. The terraced after decks and their swimming pools, originally reserved for tourist class, swept from the base of the funnels nearly into the sea. And her wrap-around Boat Deck, nestled below her lifeboats and tenders, was one of the very best.

Different opinions and appraisals of the new P&O-Orient superliners continued. 'Canberra's place among post-Second World War ocean liners was uniquely alone,' said Der Scutt, the well-known New York City-based architect and chairman of the Ocean Liner Council at that City's South Street Seaport Museum. 'The P&O management was always at the forefront of building larger, more efficient ships with increasingly greater comfort. During the war, for example, one-half of the P&O fleet was sunk. Consequently, P&O's direction was to rebuild and be second to none.'

'Later, perhaps the completion of Oriana a half-year before Canberra was a good thing because Oriana may have been one of the ugliest passenger ships ever constructed,' added Scutt. 'The stack position in the center of the vessel atop a pile of confusion certainly set the ship apart as being uniquely grotesque. Oriana's stern appeared as a beehive of unanswered openings. General fenestration above the lifeboats was inconsistent and randomly articulated. However, there were hints in the general exterior arrangement of Oriana that probably contributed to the subsequent, magnificent styling of Canberra.'

'Canberra's exterior was a unified composition of form and style with a consistent arrangement of vertical window fenestration on all decks,' concluded Scutt on the subject of exterior design. 'While the stacked bridge structure was completely different from most ocean liners of the time, it nevertheless presented a quickly recognizable profile. The twin stacks were correctly positioned toward the aft end of the ship in relation to the engine and generator rooms, boiler plant and propulsion equipment area, which was purposely kept away from passenger areas to avoid inconvenient noise and vibration. The cruiser stern with its fenestration completed the sleekness of the overall ship styling, and as such, advanced a more gracious "ship image" over the Oriana.'

'Both Canberra and Oriana had distinctive knuckles, which added to the image of speed. Canberra's knuckle, however, seemed to be integrated into the ship's hull much better and with a pleasing line. And the recessed lifeboat bays were certainly a forerunner to today's cruise ships, and represented one of the earliest such configurations. The structural columns in each lifeboat bay were carried to the Arena Deck in a pleasing and consistent set of proportions.'

P&O was, of course, one of Britain's finest and best-known shipping companies, and one with a long, distinguished, colorful, even romantic history. Created in 1837, P&O started as the Peninsular Steam Navigation Company, trading from Falmouth to Portugese and Spanish ports on the Iberian peninsular. Within two years, the new Company was trading to the Eastern Mediterraneam, to Egypt, and, by 1840, was retitled as P&O, Peninsular & Oriental. Steady progress followed including the organization of the first cruise in 1844. Their passengers grew in increasing size as well as luxury. The Valetta was, in 1884, for example, the first P&O ship with electric light. In 1914, P&O merged with British India, creating a combined fleet of 197 ships. P&O bought 51 per cent of the rival Orient Line four years later and, by the mid-1920s, had a combined fleet of over 500 ships. The New Zealand Shipping Company and Federal Steam Navigation were also now part of the P&O empire. The remaining shares of the Orient Line were acquired in 1961 and, a decade later, over 100 subsidiaries were reorganized into far fewer units. The passenger division, P&O-Princess Cruises, became a separate unit in 2000 and itself was purchased by Miami-based Carnival Corporation in 2004.

The P&O and the Orient lines were widely known in passenger shipping. Both had well-known passenger fleets. 'There was a feeling in Australia that the rival Orient Line and its liners were slightly superior to their greatest British-flag rival, the P&O Line,' recalled Tony Ralph, an avid passenger ship enthusiast who lived in Sydney in the 1960s. 'The Orient Line's staff even felt they were better than those on the P&O liners. Orient ships had grill rooms in first class, for example, and even charged an extra tariff. Also, Orient liners were decorated by Brian O'Rourke, a talented New Zealander, who used very contemporary styles. This gave the ships greater character. It was actually very functional, but at the same time an elegant style that was ideally suited for the tropics. Comparatively, the P&O liners were heavier, more English in décor. Orient Line leaned to a lighter, more free Australian taste.'

'Canberra's interiors were all of a piece,' according to Charles Howland. 'They were ultra-modern for their time and, as far as I know, very popular with the traveling public. It is always rather dangerous to use the term timeless, but I felt her public rooms stood the test of time.'

Others had different opinions. Brad Hatry said, 'Canberra's original interiors, particularly in tourist class, were quite stark and took some getting used to by those of us weaned on North Atlantic liners. Her first class furnishings were better, but very light in design, superbly comfortable for those long stretches at sea. The Canberra had a plethora of public rooms to accommodate her 2,000-plus passengers. All flowed nicely from one end to the next, but better, in most cases, onboard the Oriana. To me, Oriana had the superior interiors, much more akin to the liners we'd been accustomed to on the North Atlantic: warm, cozy, lots of paneling, more traditional. Unfortunately, there were no "grand" spaces aboard the Canberra – no sweeping ballroom, no double-height ceilings, no grand stairwells. In later years and after multiple refurbishments, however, the Canberra's décor softened and she became more akin to a fine British hotel.'

'I boarded the Canberra for the first time on 10 February 1973 and was instantly mesmerized by her unique beauty,' said architect/liner collector

Robert Allen. 'Long before the QE2's "epic spiral staircase", the Canberra's "floating spiral staircase" connecting the forward first class accommodation was a triumph. I still recall being dazzled by the white stone steps, illuminated by a continuous light strip in the solid curving banister, surrounded by walls of dark wood. This was an absolutely unique shipboard interior, unlike anything seen before or since. At the top of the spiral stair with superb 180-degree views, the intimately-sized Crow's Nest is the most favorite observation lounge that I have experienced. Equally impressive was the first class Bonito Club, still in my top ten favorite post-war liner lounges. With its beautiful wood paneling, huge "sunken living room" central section and aft glass wall that could be opened to the pool surround, this was one of the most pleasant rooms that I have ever enjoyed at sea. The freshness, unique lighting, color and quality of furnishings of these rooms was consistent throughout the ship.'

Stanley Haviland of Sydney traveled on the Canberra for the first time in 1994, when the ship was in fact nearing the end of her days. 'Traveling on her from Sydney to Perth gave me my first time to enjoy her interiors,' he recalled, 'but my fare gave me the pleasure of the old tourist class dining room, the Atlantic. Although she was now a one-class ship, it still gave you the feeling of two classes when compared to the upper Pacific Dining Room. The lino had faded from my earlier visits, for example, but my impressions of her were that she just got better as she aged. With many upgrades and refits, and a new lease on life after the Falklands War, the en suite facilities improved, even if you had to sit sidesaddle on some of the new add-on bathrooms.'

Architect Der Scutt was less impressed. 'The interiors of the Canberra, however, for me, represented a kind of sterile banality. It is true that the ship's designers were experimenting with new materials such as mural "vynide", which were durable and easily maintained wall coverings that came in decorative colors. Similarly, the use of improved "marble" linoleum flooring, sometimes in pattern and sometimes in stripes, were used extensively. Only the colored patterned fabrics employed in the draperies, bedspreads and occasional upholstery saved the interiors from being totally clinical.'

'There was obviously far too much preoccupation with the architectural look and building designs of the 1960s, where Florence Knoll and others made architectural interiors more attractive. It is one thing to be influenced in an unimaginative way, and quite another to copy a style which is inappropriate in nautical design; Canberra certainly epitomized the lost opportunity. Supermarket interiors do little to promote fun, comfort and pleasure. Perhaps the Italian designers learned from this result when they designed the elegant Michelangelo and Raffaello (completed in 1965). On the reverse, it is also possible that the P&O designers were unduly influenced by the sterility of the SS United States.'

'Interior design aside, the Canberra was a magnificent ocean liner, whose image was different and distinctive from all other liners in existence at the time,' concluded Scutt. 'Her exterior profile and styling has contributed much to the current design philosophies of today's cruise ships.'

The Canberra was much a ship of 1960s design and décor. She reflected the large, open, bright spaces then being favored not only for some passenger ships, but for hotels, offices, schools and even home décor. Altogether, she had ten passenger decks: Sun at the top and then Games, A, B, Promenade, C, D, E, F and G. Her general amenities included full air-conditioning, stabilizers, three outdoor pools plus a paddling pool for children, a gymnasium, discotheque facilities, a theatre, children's playroom, several gift shops, a beauty salon and a barber shop. Her public rooms, which were often thoughtfully given Australian-linked names, included the Crow's Nest Bar, Bonito Club, Card Room, Island Room, Alice Springs Bar, Century Bar, Meridian Room, William Fawcett Room, Library, Writing Room, Cricketer's Tavern, Peacock Room and the Atlantic and Pacific Dining Rooms.

Passenger accommodations were diverse, meeting the needs of a full range of sea travelers – from wealthy corporate types, for example, to migrants sharing in budget quarters. There were four Verandah Suites, all doubles, located on C Deck. Each consisted of a bedroom, sitting area and a full bathroom. Also on C Deck were eight Deluxe Cabins, again all doubles, and consisting of a bedroom and bathroom. Otherwise, general cabins were arranged on seven decks: A, B, C, D, E, F and G. They had 1-4 berths and about half had private shower and toilet. Her outdoor spaces were among the largest for any ship at that time.

The late Frank Andrews, a native of Melbourne and a keen ship observer, was impressed with the Canberra's interiors. 'The Meridian Lounge was very spacious and had a great sense of flow,' he noted. 'It was the focal point of first class public spaces. It connected to the library and writing room, but also to the cozy Century Park and to a spiral staircase, one of the ship's most noted features.'

'The Bonito Club facing onto the swimming pool on Games Deck was well designed and, with retractable glass walls, could be an enclosed or open space. This was practical for both day and night uses, but also useful for changes in climates on the ship's diverse routes. It was done by Sir Hugh Casson, the very noted British designer,' added Andrews. 'Another great feature and one done by Casson was the impressive spiral staircase, which rose three decks and which were uniquely lighted by concealed fluorescent. The dining rooms were full width, but inside spaces. The Pacific Dining Room was especially notable in having bright, daytime as well as subdued evening lighting schemes. The largest spaces of all, the William Fawcett Room and Island Room, were simpler in style since they were for tourist class. The Cricketer's Tavern, cleverly themed to cricket, had a long, almost railroad car feel to it. It proved very, very popular. Another distinctive feature was the so-called court cabins where cabins 'shared' daylight from windows at the end of a passage. In all, the *Canberra* was an important ship for her age and this included her decoration.'

'The *Canberra* was, of course, revolutionary in her day,' according to Captain Nick Carlton, who served aboard both the *Canberra* and the *Oriana*. 'She had the unique turbo-electric machinery that gave her flexibility and which allowed us to control speed better in places like Suez. She was, however, not as maneuverable as P&O and her bridge officers would have liked. The *Oriana* was superior in this way. Remembering, of course, that we used tugs and berthed only in larger ports in those days. Today's ships are far different. They rarely, if ever, use tugs and can berth in some of the most remote ports.'

'The *Canberra* had some bad luck in her early years with breakdowns and disrupted schedules and bad publicity over this,' added Carlton. 'That aura sort of stayed with her. I recall seeing her during her maiden voyage at Aden in June 1961. She had had a temporary "blackout" and so there was this huge silhouette – absolutely no lights! Within the Company, the *Oriana* was always the preferred ship of the two. I think also that Orient Line had more style, better décor and generally better passenger layout.'

'The *Oriana* also had better rapport with staff and passengers as well as between the two. The *Canberra* suffered from what we called "*Canberraitis*". She was always a bit of a problem and she tended to change staff, particularly officers, who seemed isolated and remote in that top-deck "pyramid",' continued Carlton.

'Of course, the major issue with the *Canberra* was her draft problem. Quite simply, all the weight was in the stern,' noted Carlton. 'This was always countered with ballast and over the years she actually bent a full 12in. With draft, you always subtract 6in each end. "Hogging" is the term or an alternate would be "sagging". Also, from her initial design, the mechanicals on the *Canberra* are too far aft. Harland & Wolff warned P&O management and designers of this, but London wanted a futuristic design with funnels and machinery far aft. Even in later years, the *Oriana* was better suited to South Pacific cruising from Australia because she was more maneuverable and had a lighter draft.'

The prototype model of the *Canberra* as shown in 1959, two years before her completion. Some changes were made. (Richard Faber Collection)

Gleaming in all-white, the *Canberra* is seen here on trials in the spring of 1961. (P&O)

The new flagship was a modern, innovative ship. (P&O)

Following the likes of Holland America's *Rotterdam* of 1959, the *Canberra* dispensed with the conventional funnel and instead had her uptakes paired and placed aft. (P&O)

3

THREE TO 103 DAYS

'When the *Canberra* arrived in Southampton in preparation for her maiden voyage, I cannot remember whether or not I saw her,' recalled ocean liner author David Hutchings. 'But we usually had a good view of passing vessels coming in from eastward from our school room in Cowes on the Isle of Wight. We had watched, secretly from beneath our text books so as not to get an admonition from the teacher, the *Rotterdam* for the first time [1959] from that vantage point. However, for once in my life, I decided to play truant from school and travel to Southampton to see the *Canberra* off on her maiden voyage, on 2 June 1961 – my final year at school. P&O ships were by now regular callers to Southampton (in the past, they customarily used the London Docks), but their huge, all-white hulls were still an almost new, unique thrill for use shoreside admirers. The corn hulls of the Orient Line were also a delight to see. The following is taken from my notes written on that June day:

Went over (from Cowes to Southampton's Royal Pier) on *Vecta* (Red Funnel ferry). 12:45 boat. *Prins der Nederlanden* anchored off Cowes. *Gatcombe* tendering. *PdN's* hull painted white – it was black the last time I saw her. (Various other ships also described.) *Ivernia* came in sometime during the afternoon.

In the New Docks: *Canberra* (P&O-Orient Lines) ready for maiden voyage at 4:00 p.m. at new terminal in New Docks. *Pretoria Castle* and *Capetown Castle* (both Union Castle) at berth 98 and 96 ... at bows of *Capetown Castle* and ready for Southampton Regatta tomorrow (3rd).

Bought 5s (25p) ticket for *Southampton Belle* to see *Canberra* depart on her maiden voyage at 4:00 p.m. Went by other ships in New Docks and then by *Canberra*. Passengers onboard waved to us. We later learned that her sailing schedule had been altered to 5:00 p.m. so we sailed about for a bit, the skipper cracking jokes, etc. Keith Beken's (the famed maritime photographer from Cowes) green launch was moored alongside the tug *Formby* at the bows of *Canberra* and Beken Jr. (Beken Sr. – Frank – was still in charge of the firm at that time) was talking to the tug's skipper.

At 5:00 p.m., tugs pulled *Canberra* away from the quay and she blew a bass note on her siren (although later she changed to an electric siren, which sounded like 1,000 cars' hooters blowing at once). There were hundreds of people on the quay and on the sightseers' balcony of the new terminal, and along the side of the terminal in big, white letters on a blue background was 'GOOD LUCK *CANBERRA*'.

The liner was in a disgusting state really for a maiden voyage as a large belt of oil was along her starboard waterline. That had been there for 3 days and had not been cleaned off since, so the *Southampton Belle's* skipper said.

The *Canberra* was not bedecked with bunting as the *Windsor Castle* had been (on her maiden departure in August 1960) although the five tugs were and the *Pretoria Castle* and *Capetown Castle* were a bit (sic). The *Pretoria Castle* had been in (port) for a week or so and (subsequently) had no steam, but managed a wonky blast on her siren. The *Capetown Castle* had arrived that morning and managed to blow. A train whistle sounded and several cars blew their sirens and people on the terminal cheered. Two or three tugs nosed her down stream until one tug was left to direct her, but she cast off when by (abeam) the Ocean Terminal.

The *Southampton Belle* had to stay on the *Canberra*'s starb'd side due to an incident which the skipper had with the *Mauretania* the year before.

People on the Royal Pier, Mayflower Park and Ocean Terminal cheered as the *Canberra* passed them (by). I took several photos of her coming toward us (I had borrowed my brother's treasured Kodak Brownie camera that seemed to have half a marble as a lens!), but I wish I had saved one film (frame) for a complete stern view.

After all (of) her publicity, this new super, luxury, modern liner was one hour late after her widely publicized schedule!

The weather did come over cloudy but luckily turned out sunny as the *Canberra* left (the late afternoon sunshine was scorching, if I remember correctly), the sun glinting on her white hull and (twin) buff funnels.

When I had arrived (earlier) at So'ton I saw in a book stall on the Royal Pier a large pile of souvenir magazines about the *Canberra* entitled *Maiden Voyage*, but I never (sic) bought one then as I didn't want to carry one about. Just before I left Southampton I went to buy one and instead of a large pile there were (just) two copies left! (I still have mine.)

Came home on the *Vecta*. *Prins der Nederlanden* had gone. Flags still flying on (Cowes) Parade – thought for *Canberra* but obviously for the Queen's Coronation anniversary.

'In those days, maiden voyages did not seem to attract the attention that they do now,' added David Hutchings. 'If there were crowds, they consisted mostly of locals, relatives of those traveling and a few 'ship spotters' – enthusiasts – or 'buffs' as they are colloquially referred to now.'

Enthusiasm and fanfare ran high, however, when the 27-knot *Canberra* went off on her sell-out maiden voyage, an around-the-world trip in that summer of 1961. She was also the largest liner to sail from Britain to Australia & New Zealand, and then continue up to North America – to Vancouver, San Francisco and Los Angeles. Fares varied for her diverse voyages, from three to 103 days, and were appealing even then: $10 per person per day in the lowest tourist class cabin and then to about $30 a day up in first class.

On 1 June 1961, Captain Geoffrey Wild was made Commodore of the P&O fleet, a vast company then with some fifty ships in all. As master of the new flagship, he set sail with her on the following afternoon, bound for Australia with 2,238 passengers onboard. Immigrants would also be a part of her economic life for the foreseeable future and so there were 750 settlers onboard bound for Australia and 120 headed for new lives in New Zealand. Triumphant and gleaming, the *Canberra* headed for Gibraltar and then into the western Mediterranean for Naples. Later, en route to Port Said, she passed one of P&O's oldest liners, the *Strathaird*, completed in 1931-32, and the two ships exchanged warm and cordial greetings. 'You look magnificent,' flashed the veteran *Strathaird*.

But there were problems below. There was an issue with leakage in the condenser tubing. Saline had been found in the distilled water, probably caused by leakages that might trigger serious problems that eventually could seriously damage the high-powered boilers. She was slowed and then missed her place in the southbound Suez Canal convoy. This then resulted in a fourteen-hour delay at Aden and where the new liner had a complete power failure. The Red Sea heat was sweltering and, in consideration, P&O pursers invited passengers to sleep on deck for the night. She was twelve hours late at Colombo and then speed had to be reduced on the leg to Fremantle, Melbourne and then Sydney. 'There were huge crowds along the shoreline and inner waterfronts even though she was twenty-four hours late into Sydney,' recalled Tony Ralph. P&O announced that the faulty condenser has been repaired, that all was well and that the *Canberra* was in proper, well-running form. There was a forty-eight-hour delay at Auckland because of thick fog, but then more ceremonies, high-spirited maiden arrival receptions on her maiden trip along the upper Pacific – at Honolulu, Vancouver, San Francisco and Los Angeles.

She returned to Sydney and then sailed homeward on her return maiden voyage via Colombo, Aden, the Suez Canal and Gibraltar. In all, she had carried 11,000 passengers on her maiden passages, had 50,000 visitors and steamed 42,000 miles in all.

'P&O liners were remote to New Yorkers like myself, but I first saw and had the good fortune to visit the *Canberra* in Naples, Italy, on the return trip to Southampton of her maiden voyage, in August 1961,' recalled Captain Ed Squire. '*Canberra*, I thought, had beautiful lines and those twin stacks aft made her look not only futuristic, but like a big yacht – a white sea goddess. Onboard, her modern and brightly lit interiors overwhelmed me. The layout as well as the colors of the public rooms, the dining areas and the passenger cabins were quite different when compared to other British ships of prior years. Later, I saw the *Oriana* for the first time, but found her accommodations to be more subdued. She had, of course, the traditional Orient Line corn-colored hull as well. But on the *Canberra*, the unique location and recessed position on lower B Deck of the lifeboats also impressed me.'

But her woes seem to continue. There was a fire in the engine while she was preparing to sail from Southampton on 2 September. The fire was extinguished, but the departure delayed by five hours. Then, during the voyage out to Australia, a blade in one of the turbo-generators snapped and forced a 5kt reduction in speed. She made Melbourne and Sydney at a reduced 22kt.

It was in fact her fourth voyage to Australia, departing on 19 April 1962, that was her most troublesome. There were problems with her boilers as well as her distilling plant and main turbo generators. P&O worried and so later decided to revise the ship's itinerary. The return home via Australia and the Suez route was canceled and instead she was routed on the shorter run via the Panama Canal and the Caribbean. It was her first passage through the Canal, a tight squeeze in fact with only 3ft 6in of clearance on each side. The transit fee amounted to just under £11,500. But on the way home to Southampton, the air-conditioning system failed yet again and once more passengers were invited to sleep on deck for several nights.

When the *Canberra* arrived at Southampton on 21 June, a twenty-nine-day overhaul was arranged. The sheltered games area on Games Deck, between the Bonito Club and the Crow's Nest, was permanently closed over and made into a theatre. It had not proved popular as a games area. Extra air-conditioning units and equipment were added, but the overall system was never quite adequate for the ship, especially in warmer climates. The air-conditioning often strained considerably. Also, two 5ft-high extensions were added to the funnels, giving them a somewhat improved, finished look.

Afterward, the *Canberra* returned to service, making cruises as well as line voyages. In the summer of 1962, she made a special cruise from Southampton to New York and back, and had three days at Cunard Line's West 52nd Street berth as a hotel for her roundtrip guests. This was a comfortable base for their land tours. A second, highly successful cruise to New York followed, the first P&O cruises to New York since the *Arcadia* and *Iberia* crossed the North Atlantic in 1959.

There were some blemishes, however, in the otherwise dazzling early period of the *Canberra*'s career. In 1963, she had a major mechanical breakdown while outbound in the western Mediterranean. She was power-less, the entire trip had to be aborted and her future schedules disrupted. She even had to go back to her builders for repairs, to the illustrious Harland & Wolff Shipyard at Belfast.

On 4 January 1963, with 2,222 passengers onboard, the *Canberra* was steaming east in the Mediterranean at 27kt when, at four in the morning and at some 160 miles northeast of Malta, one of the three turbo-generators went on overload. As the generator began to motor, the circuit breaker failed, which caused a fire that totally destroyed the starboard side of the switchboard and the main distribution cables. With no electric power, the engines could not run, there was no lighting or ventilation or power in the galley. Parts of the lower decks became filled with smoke. Passengers were ordered to their lifeboat stations, but just as a precaution. The fire was under control within an hour.

Fortunately, another P&O liner, the 23,000-ton *Stratheden*, was homeward in the eastern Mediterranean, bound from Port Said for London, and was quickly diverted to assist her new, big fleetmate. Within hours, she was alongside and supplying the stricken *Canberra* with bread and other supplies. Two British warships, HMS *Lion* and HMS *Scorpion*, were sent to assist and Shackleton AEW aircraft based on Malta were dispatched to overfly the P&O flagship.

Within hours, there were headlines in all the British newspapers as well as television and radio reports, and emergency planning at P&O's London headquarters. One headline read, 'Drama Off Malta'. Of course, the voyage to Australia was aborted. A young, up-and-coming air transport specialist named Freddie Laker was placed in charge of 'Malta Airlift'. Within a day, no less than fourteen large aircraft were chartered by P&O and some 1,700 passengers were flown onward to their destinations in Australia and New Zealand.

'I was with the US Navy, aboard the USS *Grand Canyon*, when we arrived at Malta two days after the stricken *Canberra* arrived,' remembered Captain Ed Squire. 'We were anchored a short distance from the P&O flagship and later met some of the *Canberra*'s crew, including some of her engineers, while ashore. They invited us aboard and to see the damages to the electrical system. We climbed about *Canberra*'s main engine, boiler spaces and electrical area. The damage from the fire was extensive and destroyed much of the electrical wiring and switchboard that controlled the ship's main lighting and turbo-electric propulsion system. What was of special interest to me, however, was how far aft her machinery was located. *Canberra*'s three main boilers were aft of the maintenance room and due to the extensive weight of the boilers, the *Canberra* had a deep draft of 35½ft. The captain and chief engineer told us that she had a bend in her keel as a result. Later, the bent keel played a role in her grounding during Caribbean cruises from New York in 1973.'

Within ten days, with temporary repairs made in Malta and with forty-six passengers, who preferred to remain onboard, the *Canberra* headed for Belfast, her builders' yard and full, lengthy repairs. The voyage took seven days, which included a stint facing 60kt winds. The repairs took 3½ months and included the installation of a new switchboard as well as a general overhaul. There were final repairs and adjustments made at Southampton before, on 24 May, the ship left Southampton on another voyage to Australia. Unaffected by the harsh publicity, she set off with a record 2,265 passengers.

'For all of her days, the *Canberra* was cantankerous in ways,' recalled one of her junior officers, later Captain Martin Reed. 'She didn't listen to commands very well and often went in the opposite direction. And it was well known that she was 15ft lower in the stern from the day of launching. The forward hold, intended for cargo, was made into a permanent ballast tank, which brought the bow down. Once, we tried to bend her back while in dry dock, but then the decks became uneven and many doors would not close. We actually had to bend her back, keeping that 15ft drop in the stern!'

All seemed well for the most part during the 1960s for P&O-Orient and their passenger fleet. The *Canberra* and *Oriana* became two of the best known, most popular liners afloat. Even Americans grew to favor them. There were differences between the ships, of course, and Dean Miller recalled these. 'P&O had staff captains on their liners, for example, whereas Orient liners had staff commanders. The Orient Line ships were perhaps slightly more prestigious and compared more favorably to the celebrated Atlantic liners of those years. The *Orcades*, *Oronsay* and *Orsova* each had a special first class grill room that was placed aft and looked out over the stern section from floor-to-ceiling windows. There was an extra fee for admittance, even for first class passengers, but this was quite modest even in those days. There was more variety in the grill room menu selection, perhaps even better service than the actual first class restaurants and certainly lots more caviar and special desserts. We used these grill rooms for our press functions and receptions during the customary two-day layovers in Vancouver.'

'By the early 1960s, in less than ten years of service, it became unusual to embark anything less than 1,000 passengers at Vancouver on these P&O-Orient liners. This was a great record for Vancouver in those days, certainly long before the current boom days of the Alaskan cruise trade. Then, beginning in 1961, the giant *Oriana* and *Canberra* were added. On these liners, we customarily embarked 1,500 passengers per sailing. This great prosperity would continue for at least another decade, until the early 1970s,' added Miller.

Joann Hastings, later entertainment director for the ultra-luxurious, San Francisco-based Seabourn Cruise Lines, was employed at Orient & Pacific in 1958. 'We actually had only a back room at Cunard's San Francisco office. Cunard kept the very elegant front office space,' she recalled. 'We had two representatives from London, one for P&O and one for the Orient Line. It was very interesting, certainly a unique operation and there were lots of colorful characters there who had lots of tales and stories to tell. It was all very exciting, especially to someone on her first job!'

In the mid-1960s, Joann left what was then the Post Street offices of a retitled, expanded P&O-Orient Lines and escorted groups of Americans on trips aboard these otherwise essentially British liners. 'On these trips, we really were not cruising in the contemporary sense,' she fondly noted. 'These were 'line voyages' only. They were voyages of pure transport, taking passengers from Point A to Point B. I especially remember a trip on the *Orsova*, a six-month voyage completely around the world. I escorted 150 Americans and we sailed from San Francisco to Australia and then to the Suez Canal and Mediterranean. We left the ship at Naples to do some overland European touring before re-joining the ship in London. But our six-month journey turned into nine months! We reached London just in time for the big, six-week British maritime strike [Spring 1966] and so our three nights in a London hotel turned into six weeks! P&O had to pay all the extra hotel bills. Our group had shrunk to fifty when the strike was over and the *Orsova* was finally ready to sail on 4 July for San Francisco. By way of the Caribbean and Panama, it took another three weeks to get home.'

'We often marketed these line voyages as "cruises" and even gave them names like "Jolly Swagman" and "Waltzing Mathilda". Sometimes they ran up to 125 days. Our American passengers tended to be older, usually retired and often great characters, even eccentrics, in themselves. They traveled in both classes and I was their link for all ship's matters and for their shore tours.'

Joann sailed on other P&O-Orient liners including the *Canberra* and *Oriana*, which were sensibly advertised as the two largest liners afloat apart from the North Atlantic superliners. 'I especially remember all of these ships for their onboard smells, the smells of British cooking, that ever-prevailing odor of cooked cabbage,' she added. 'But sailing in many of them was all part of a glorious youthful experience – such as my first full exposure to Indian curries and over-cooked vegetables, and to go down the hall to the toilet and to a separate room for a bath.'

Spanning the globe, voyages ranged from three to 103 days. Thick Company brochures often romantically suggested 'Runaway to sea with P&O'. Living in San Francisco and later on Maui in Hawaii, Ginger Fortin often did. The 709ft-long *Oronsay*, a two-class ship completed in 1951, was her first P&O-Orient voyage. The year was 1960. 'I was a teacher at the time and so it was a summer vacation trip on the *Oronsay*, from San Francisco to Honolulu by way of Vancouver. There were lots of American as well as Canadian passengers onboard. I was in first class with my parents and which seemed pleasant. But there were no other young people and so I was soon very bored. Each day was quite quiet, almost sedate. The captain, other officers and the general crew clashed and so the mood onboard was down, often stressful. It ruined me, as a young person, for traveling in first class in the future. The great fun, I believed thereafter, was in tourist class. But I do recall that the food, even in first class on the *Oronsay*, was quite awful. The beef, for example, was un-chewable. Later, I would come to believe that first class food on P&O was the equivalent of tourist class food on Cunard, which of course was also British. I must say, however, that following the P&O and Orient Line merger, the food on the combined ships did improve somewhat.'

'I have many memories of my many voyages in the *Canberra*,' said Linette Reynolds. 'In the mornings, there was always a continental breakfast delivered at a set time or close to it by a steward, often one of the Goanese. Then there was the parade of sorts, usually in bathrobes and slippers, to the public bathrooms that had these enormous tubs. This was followed by a full breakfast in one of the two dining rooms. Much of the day was then spent on deck, resting, reading or sunning in one of those collapsible wood and canvas deckchairs. They could cause quite a fuss, even a big problem, if you were unfamiliar with the unfolding and set-up. Many a bruised or cut finger resulted with first timers. Deck games were serious business – shuffleboard and deck tennis and, most serious of all, a deck cricket match between officers and crew. Luncheons including occasional buffets were often highlighted by the most magnificent curries anywhere. They were legendary on P&O and had been for decades, of course, and well worth their reputation. The *Canberra*, like many British liners in those days, seemed to go quiet from two until four in the afternoon. Everyone was napping, either in their cabins or on deck in one of those canvas chairs. Four o'clock tea broke the spell, of course. Dressing for dinner often meant listening to *Radio Canberra*, which included shipboard news, updates, interviews with staff and perhaps a chatty but interesting fellow passenger and often funny P&O advertisements for future sailings. I recall some of these being done in a sort of 1930s drawing room style with highly affected speech, a bit of drama and then the expected humor. There might be cocktail parties or simply drinks at a bar before dinner. Most popular of all bars aboard was, however, the Crow's Nest. Dinner was the most seriously taken meal and followed a rather strict multi-course pattern. Afterward, there was dancing, films in the cinema, a quiz and, in later years, showtime productions such as *Ole' English Music Hall* and *Musicals of the West End*, and another noted event: *Island Night*, a large deck party. Well into the night, there were the old timers, the regulars, always seated in usually quiet Meridian Lounge. Many would have dozed off, often for hours at a time. But there was the opposite: the very lively atmosphere in the Cricketer's Tavern. The ship tended to go quite quiet by midnight, many

passengers tired from activities of the day and, of course, lots of sun and fresh air. It was late in the night that you could hear more of the hum of the ship's motors. It was, in its way, a reassuring sound. The *Canberra* was a welcome home, the moving city, a most wonderful ship.'

Ginger Fortin became a skilled planner of her ocean-going travels. Her teaching schedule meant that she could travel only in summer, leaving in late June and home by the beginning of September for the start of classes. 'Once, I sailed from San Francisco at the end of June on the *Orsova*,' she remembered. 'It was a seven-week sailing to Honolulu, Yokohama, Kobe, Hong Kong, Singapore, Bombay, the Suez Canal, Marseilles and then London. After Hong Kong, the great majority of passengers were British. My parents came along on the *Orsova* and paid $1,200 each for the seven weeks to London. Their first class cabin did not have a private bathroom, however. They used public showers and toilets located along the corridors. Myself, I paid $1,000 for a bunk in a tourist class six-berth. I had three hurried days ashore in London before going down to Southampton to join the *Oriana*. I returned to San Francisco on her by way of Bermuda, Nassau, Fort Lauderdale, Kingston, the Panama Canal, Acapulco and Los Angeles. I was home by Labor Day [early September], just in time to resume classes, having completed a seventy-five-day trip around the world!'

'The *Oriana* was quite different from the *Orsova*,' she noted. 'She was one of the two newest P&O-Orient liners of the 1960s. The other was, of course, the *Canberra*. The early voyages of both ships were often especially big events. Welcoming ceremonies, flags and banners flying, arrival escorts of tugs, pleasure boats and even spraying fireboats, bands playing, newspaper headlines and then a gala open house to the locals. The *Oriana* was a very impressive ship for that time, at nearly 42,000 tons and carrying over 2,000 passengers. She was, however, a very comfortable ship in first class, but far less so in tourist class. All doors and barriers between first and tourist class were locked by six in the evening and so I needed a special pass if I wanted to join my parents for dinner up in first class.'

'The passengers changed in every port on these P&O-Orient "line voyages" as they called them and so I met many local people,' concluded Ginger Fortin. 'There was a great sense of a "real voyage" about that *Orsova* trip. She was a wonderful ship, one of my favorites. Altogether, I did three trips on her. She was also a very friendly ship. The captain, as I recall, even attended a kids' fancy dress party in tourist class and had tea every day with my parents in first class. I celebrated my twenty-first birthday on the *Orsova*, at a dinner arranged by my parents in the first class grill room.'

In those years, P&O-Orient liners, including the *Canberra*, carried all sorts of passengers: corporate moguls and diplomats, businessmen and their families, whole sports teams and, of course, a seemingly endless flow of tourists.

According to Dean Miller, 'This was also an era when a young Australian could not hold his or her head up if he or she had not been to Britain. Even if you could fly, you didn't. So, these budget travelers filled the tourist class end of ships like the *Canberra*. Many stopped off in Vancouver and worked in Canada for three, four, even six months before continuing on to England via Panama. Others worked their way across Canada and then took Cunard or Canadian Pacific from Montreal. It was all part of a process.'

'Also, many press photographers today in Vancouver are Australians, who first came on the *Canberra*, *Oriana* and other P&O liners,' concluded Miller. 'In fact, there was a special Australian organization to meet inbound P&O liners up from Sydney and Melbourne. In reverse, we also had many Australian tourists going home, from Britain via the Panama Canal route and stopping on the Pacific West Coast. Australian passengers used these ships to the very end, to the last voyage out to Australia from Vancouver on the *Oriana* in late 1981.'

In the spring of 1966, the British passenger ship fleet was all but devasted by a six-week national maritime strike. Seamen's unions were demanding not only a shorter working week, but a 17 per cent pay increase as well. The *Canberra*, along with the *Arcadia* and other liners, sat idle along the Southampton Docks. In silent splendor, the lay-up of these ships was, in many ways, a prelude to the future. Airlines had already conquered the famed North Atlantic run, carrying as many as 95 per cent of all travelers and leaving ships such as Cunard's legendary, but aging *Queen Mary* and *Queen Elizabeth* all but empty, even in the normally peak summer months. Following the strike, and with millions in the red, Cunard announced the abrupt withdrawal of no less than five liners within twelve months. But competition from the airlines was mounting on routes east of Suez. By the late 1960s, P&O was facing a fierce, unbeatable competitor. It was quickly becoming twenty-one hours from London to Sydney rather than twenty-one days. Even the comparatively new *Canberra* and *Oriana* were losing passengers. The older ships such as the *Himalaya*, *Orcades*, *Chusan* and *Oronsay* were in far greater jeopardy – they lost passengers as well as cargo that now went in faster, more efficient container ships and would be in need of costly upgrades and modernizations to secure an economic place in the 1970s. In fact, it was the eighteen-year-old *Iberia*, plagued with operational troubles, that led the parade of P&O liners to the block. The likes of the twenty-five-year-old *Orcades* and the twenty-three-year-old *Chusan* soon followed, finishing their days after long, lonely final voyages at the hands of Taiwanese scrappers. The *Arcadia* finished this sad parade of the older, earlier P&O liners when she completed her final voyage at Kaohsiung in the spring of 1979.

A New York friend had gone home to Australia in 1972 and, having been fascinated by ships, especially liners, along the Melbourne waterfront in the 1930s, his interest was again sparked. With camera in hand, he revisited the Melbourne docks – and later the Sydney waterfront as well. A keen photographer, he captured a great collection of liners: the likes of the *Arcadia*, *Iberia*, *Himalaya*, *Cathay*, *Australis*, *Patris*, *Achille Lauro* and *Fairstar*. They were often at dock, resting between the line voyages from British and European ports. None of us, himself included, realized it was all coming to an end, that a great curtain was closing. The airlines, with their speedy jets, had finally and firmly reached out beyond Suez. The great liners of the Australian run were now great dinosaurs: struggling, short of passengers, losing lots of money. From Sydney's Pyrmont Dock, my friend captured in a series of fine photos a spirited sailing of the *Iberia*. Streamers were twisted and knotted between ship and shore, for example, and thousands lined the quayside while passengers filled the outer decks and open promenade decks of the eighteen-year-old liner. Still in middle age for liners, she was in fact on her final voyage home to the UK. She was mechanically troubled and therefore required frequent and expensive repairs, and so was selected as the first of the post-Second World War P&O-Orient liners to end her days – and all of them prematurely. Partially stripped, the still-handsome *Iberia* left Southampton in April 1972 bound for the then very hungry scrappers of Kaohsiung on Taiwan. Coincidentally, just two years earlier, in July 1970, another friend and I thought of having a P&O summer, making a three-week trip from Vancouver to San Francisco and Los Angeles, then to Acapulco and through the Panama Canal, and stopping at Kingston, Port Everglades and Bermuda before crossing the Atlantic to Southampton. With rather trim wallets, we found we could have done the voyage for $11 per person per day in a tourist class double-down on C Deck. Alas, plans changed and instead we opted for a series of shorter voyages, cruises from New York and Miami. In retrospect, it was a mistake. What great fun to have spent three weeks on the *Iberia*!

'After the Second World War, the peak years for the UK/Europe-Australia passenger trade were in the late 1940s and mid-'50s. After that, there was a settling down and then an end to it all by the early '70s,' according to Ted Birkett, who had been in the passenger ship business in Sydney for decades. 'Both the *Canberra* and the *Oriana* were actually too late. So was Shaw Savill's *Northern Star*. None of these ships would have long, economic careers on the Australian run and, of course, the two P&O-Orient liners had to turn to fulltime cruising while the *Northern Star* went to the breakers at the age of fourteen and so she was the least economic. The *Canberra* and *Oriana* were sort of the last hurrahs of the old P&O and Orient lines. The name *Oriana* was thought of in 1953 at the time of the Coronation and the name was to commemorate the twin Elizabethan generations. There was, of course, still a very strong link between Britain and Australia. *Canberra* was purely commercial in choice, in hopes of luring many more Australians onboard.'

Above: A poetic scene along the Sydney waterfront. (J & C McCutcheon Collection)

Above left: The *Canberra* arrives at Sydney for the first time on 29 June 1961. (P&O)

Left: The new flagship at Circular Quay, Sydney and in the shadows of the famed Harbor Bridge. (J & C McCutcheon Collection)

A dramatic aerial view of *Canberra* in her early years. (Author's Collection)

A latter-day view, also in the King George V Graving Dock, as *Canberra* undergoes her annual refit. (Author's Collection)

The ship takes a turn in Southampton's King George V Graving Dock. (Fred Rodriguez Collection)

Part of the 'under belly' of the great ship at Southampton. (Fred Rodriguez Collection)

Above: A stern view of *Canberra* taken at Palma de Majorca during a Mediterranean cruise. (Author's Collection)

Above right: *Canberra*'s first arrival in New York, in June 1962. (Port Authority of New York & New Jersey)

Right: Arriving at New York's Pier 92. (Fred Rodriguez Collection)

Above: The Bonito Club as completed in 1961. (P&O)

Above left: Outbound from New York on a summer's evening, June 1973. (Author's Collection)

Left: Modern interiors: the Crow's Nest Observation Lounge, 1961. (P&O)

The first class restaurant with, as the P&O caption describes, 'evening settings'. (P&O)

A verandah suite. (P&O)

The first class Games Deck, along the port side. (P&O)

Another view of the Bonito Club, but facing aft. It too is in an 'evening arrangement'. Designer Barry Banyard adds, 'A clear dance floor – with tables and chairs outside around the pool. The glass screen separating the Club and the pool is recessed into the deck.' (Barry Banyard Collection)

The *Canberra*'s interiors are today a study and reflection of mid-century design. A first class area: the top landing of the main stairwell. Barry Banyard added, 'Note the mirror on the half landing [to the left], which shows the deck below.' (Barry Banyard Collection)

Another section of the main stairwell. On the far side is an illuminated section of the ship to show passengers the position of the public rooms. (Barry Banyard Collection)

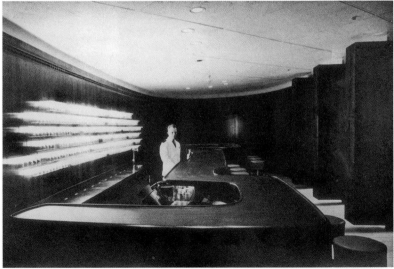

The cinema. The doors shown are to the first class section of the ship. The doors include viewing slots with such areas designated by a darker wood. (Barry Banyard Collection)

The Century Bar with ceiling spotlights that follow the shape of the bar. (Barry Banyard Collection)

Above: Glasses behind the Century Bar, all hung on perspex shelves lit from behind the paneling. (Barry Banyard Collection)

Left: Footstools in the Century Bar with tan leather seats and solid brass footrests. (Barry Banyard Collection)

More chairs along the Promenade Deck outside the Meridian Room, a first class area. Morning coffee and afternoon tea were served here. (Barry Banyard Collection)

The grand piano placed in the Meridian Room and designed by Barry Banyard. (Barry Banyard Collection)

In the Crystal Room, the ship's private first class dining room, a special case for the television was made in timber to match the walls. (Barry Banyard Collection)

Outdoor spaces abounded aboard the *Canberra*: the upper, open decks as seen in
1961. (P&O)

The midships pool area. (P&O)

A classic P&O deck scene, one dating from October 1980. (Author's Collection)

4

GOING CRUISING

P&O-Orient Lines were innovative in some ways, but the Orient Line had had some earlier innovations of their own. 'Orient offered some of the very first cruises from Australia, even as far back as the 1930s, for example,' added Tony Ralph. 'Both P&O and Orient were really very much mainline, deep-sea companies. They rarely cruised in their early years. But by the 1930s, they began to experiment, making cruises from Sydney to Auckland and Wellington, a ten-day trip in all, and later with excursions to the South Pacific islands, to the likes of Noumea and Suva. The full merger of the P&O and Orient lines in 1960 was said to be a difficult one for the Orient Line. In fact, by 1966, the Orient name was dropped altogether and ships such as the *Orcades*, *Oronsay* and *Orsova* were run thereafter as P&O liners. And by then, cruising was very much a part of the Company's annual program.

It might be rather difficult to understand that P&O managers thought seriously, in fact quite seriously, of retiring the *Canberra* in 1974 and actually selling her off, most likely to those hungry scrappers of Taiwan. The P&O flagship had lost her clientele in the two-class Australian and around-the-world trades and, in a misguided move, had just finished a largely unsuccessful nine-month stint of cruising from New York, mostly to the Caribbean. She arrived in New York for a series of cruises in January 1973. Marketing, sales and reservations were handled by Cunard's Fifth Avenue offices, but with, it seems, the effect that Cunard ships and their voyages were sold first. P&O and the *Canberra* were second choices and furthermore the ship was not as well known to the American cruising public as, say, the *Queen Elizabeth 2* or even the smallish *Cunard Adventurer* and *Cunard Ambassador*. Consequently, the *Canberra* often left her Manhattan berth on eight-fifteen-day cruises,

including one to West Africa, sometimes at only 50 per cent of her cruise capacity, which was fixed at 1,700. She was even laid-up in February-March 1973 in the Cape Fear River, near Wilmington, North Carolina. Her 960 crew occasionally used tenders to get ashore and a local fishing boat was used for mail and other supplies. And then there were further blemishes – she went aground twice in the Caribbean.

Robert Pelletier is a maritime historian and collector, but who also spent over thirty years working in the passenger ship business. 'For a portion of 1973, I was District Sales Manager for Cunard in Massachusetts, but it was not too easy to convince travel agents in New England of the uniqueness of this liner. P&O was unknown to them. Cunard, of course, were the general agents for her New York-Caribbean cruises in 1973. There were too many cabins without private facilities and they certainly had a tough time selling those court cabins to their groups. Who ever heard of an inside cabin having a view of a window, which overlooked the sea below? We had a pierside overnight for agents aboard the ship during which P&O went all out, but it was still a tough sell. It became even harder to sell after the ship ran aground twice in the Caribbean because she drew too much water at the stern.'

'While I visited the *Canberra* about fifteen times, most of these during her fateful single season of cruising from New York, I sailed aboard her only once,' recalled Brad Hatry. 'My 1973 cruise was certainly a memorable one as well. We sailed from New York on a very hot and humid Sunday afternoon, 8 July, with nearly 2,100 passengers onboard for a scheduled ten-day Caribbean cruise. After three days at sea, we arrived at our first port-of-call, Grenada. The *Canberra* overshot her anchorage and we touched a sandbar, grounded for much of the next four days. Two tugs were dispatched from Trinidad to attempt to pull the *Canberra* free, but succeeded only in keeping her from drifting harder aground. On our second day aground, a friend and I were walking on her Boat Deck, midships and on the starboard side. Suddenly, there was an earsplitting crack. We learned shortly after that one of the steel cables connecting ship to tug had snapped, the recoil crashing through the grates of the *Canberra's* aft-positioned laundry and decapitating a Goanese laundryman. During our third night aground, an oil barge arrived from St Thomas to offload fuel in an effort to lighten the *Canberra* and set her free. It worked and we spent the fourth day at Grenada afloat, but with fuel being pumped back aboard. We skipped our next scheduled port-of-call, Martinique, stopped at Barbados and St Thomas, and arrived back in New York two days late.'

'I truly liked and enjoyed the *Canberra* and could just imagine those long sea voyages from England to Australia. She had to be superb on that run for which she was designed,' added Hatry. 'But she just didn't work as a Caribbean cruise ship, particularly one based in the United States. She was too deep draft, having to anchor at nearly every port. Her many cabins without shower or toilet were unacceptable, even as far back as 1973, to most American passengers. Barely approaching middle age, the then twelve-year-old liner seemed archaic when competing with the flashy new ships then entering the US cruise market. It was impossible to believe that best years laid ahead.'

Another American ocean liner historian, Robert Allen, was aboard in 1973 as well. 'I sailed on my first-ever cruise on the *Canberra* from New York on 5 September, about three weeks before my sixteenth birthday,' he recalled. 'To say she left a great impression on me would be a huge understatement! Besides the excitement of finally sailing on an ocean liner, I recall the ship having great warmth as well as a fun, cozy feeling. Sailing out of New York on that muggy September evening, I recall that the first class pool was already filled and so I took a late night dip to celebrate the start of my first cruise. I was assigned to the first class dining room – a grounding accident in late August, followed by a delayed sailing date resulted in an upgrade. The hushed elegance of the room (with lighting designed to change the room's mood from morning to noon to evening), superb service by a Goanese steward and an exotic menu made for a memorable dining experience. Buffets and barbecues on deck were fun and lighthearted. I recall inquiring what some sliced meat was on the midnight buffet (held in the open-air Stadium), and receiving the answer "pressed Yak"! Teatime was in the Bonito Club – with glass screens open to the pool on a balmy Caribbean afternoon – was delightful. I could almost imagine we were gliding through the Suez

Canal en route to Australia! My outside single cabin off a D Deck forward "courtyard" was appropriately "posh", and my very charming British steward told me stories of his wartime maiden voyage crossing on the *Queen Elizabeth* in 1940. In summary, this was a great ship and great cruise experience that I shall never forget.'

In September 1973, the *Canberra* made a one-way trip home, from New York to Southampton. Her future seemed uncertain, even bleak. A year later, in September 1974, another money-losing super liner, the *France*, was withdrawn and the Italians announced that their twin super ships, *Michelangelo* and *Raffaello*, would be retired soon afterward. The future for liners, especially big ones, was dim. Among other problems, the cost of fuel oil had suddenly and dramatically soared from $35 to $95 a ton. Home office accountants, including those at P&O in London, were deeply worried. The fuel-hungry *Canberra* was worth, it was reported, £600,000 if sold for scrap, but more if sold to other owners. There was a possibility, according to London sources, that she might undergo a costly process – being re-engined to more efficient diesel. The price for that procedure was fixed around £3 million. But that nagging problem of her draft persisted. She drew 35½ft of water, but needed to draw 32ft when entering some of the more shallow cruise ports.

The *Canberra* was now a misfit, a costly dinosaur. Yes, P&O looked to something of a future in one-class cruising, but those London managers thought at first of refitting the 29,000-ton, 1954-built *Orsova*. With some 1,400 berths, she would be adequate or so they thought. Fortunately, some re-thinking prevailed – and the *Canberra* was saved. She even had a ten-week refit, making her more suitable as a one-class ship. One children's playroom was eliminated and made over as the Card Room while the Letter Bureau on A Deck became the Kiosk and later the Boutique. The Writing Room on the Promenade Deck also had a re-doing and became the William Fawcett Shop (and later the Ocean Shop). Furthermore, some four-berth cabins were restyled as doubles.

'The *Orsova* was to do the world cruise in January 1974,' recalled the late Frank Jackson, a noted P&O port lecturer and shore excursions staff member. 'But just before, she had a nasty outbreak of dysentery while on a Mediterranean cruise and consequently had some very bad press back home in the UK. The *Canberra* had been scheduled to go to the breakers in the Far East. She had deep draft problems and was a great liability to P&O. But the Company reversed the ships and the *Canberra* made the world voyage. She was saved. It was a foggy, miserable night at Southampton when instead the *Orsova* sailed away to the breakers. Sadly, there was no one there to see her. It was all unscheduled. The *Orsova* departed in the mist, with no sentimental send-off, but her whistle kept going just the same.'

The *Canberra* settled down to a sensible pattern: nine months of mostly two- and three-week cruises from Southampton and then, in January, a three-month cruise around the world. The *Oriana* operated with her, but left for Australia in November and joined the *Arcadia* at Sydney for several months of Pacific cruising before returning to the UK in spring. It all seemed the right decision – P&O Cruises lost nearly £7 million in 1975, but showed a profit of over £4 million in the following year. Happily, cruising was becoming increasingly popular in Britain.

Frank Jackson and his wife Evelyn had been aboard every *Canberra* world cruise since 1974. 'We had 1,000 passengers making the full three-month trip in 1974,' Frank Jackson noted. 'By 1986, about 300 were making the complete voyage. We would give as many as three and sometimes four lectures a day. These would be on the ports of call, on regional history, but also about Britain itself. We would do three topics just on London and five or six on British geography and history. We also did talks on European capitals as well. We traveled with 85-90,000 slides. I once tried to get them insured, but Lloyd's quoted me £1 per slide, which meant an annual premium of £90,000! We also did "Can We Help You" lectures and the questions afterward were often fascinating. These included: "My top plate has broken and where can I find a dentist?" to "Can I change *draculas* in Greece?" to "When will they finally clean up the bomb damage at the Acropolis?"'

Frank and Evelyn Jackson began their P&O lecture careers on the likes of the old *Strathmore* in the 1950s and later served on ships such as the *Arcadia*, *Chusan* and *Cathay*. They had seen great differences and changes in their sea-going years that spanned some forty years in all. 'By the 1980s, cruising was within the means of so many more British travelers,' they said. 'Incomes had increased, especially between the 1950s and the 1980s. Earlier, many of these same people would not even think of going beyond British holiday camps or seaside resorts such as Blackpool and Bournemouth. On the earlier cruises, even onboard the *Canberra*, there was much less entertainment then. Passengers were content with a dance band and a coffee in the lounge. Even up until the 1960s, ships "went to sleep" in the afternoons. Everyone napped, or so it seemed, between two and four. But as younger travelers appeared onboard, those naps gave way more and more to games at the pool and other activities. There were the same changes in Australia, for sailings and even cruises out of Sydney. In the 1950s, we had mostly well-to-do Australians, older and more sedate. But it quickly became younger people in shorts and thongs and with long, sticky hair. The boys used girls' tights as streamers! And they all seemed to have knapsacks on their backs!'

Generally, the *Canberra* was used on continuous two- and three-week cruises out of Southampton and then, from January through April, made a three-month trip around the world. I did four trips aboard her, between 1980 and 1983, as a guest lecturer, talking about great passenger ships past and present. The audiences, often numbering up to 4-500, sometimes arrived thirty minutes early to ensure a good seat. At the conclusion of each fifty-minute talk, there was a flood of questions, stories and anecdotes to share. One lady sent me her collection of menus from the old *Aquitania* and another gentleman forwarded all his keepsakes from annual cruises beginning in 1932. Another dear soul sent a dozen silver-plated trophy cups that she had won from various deck games and tournaments onboard the likes of the *Southern Cross*, *Chusan* and *Kenya Castle*.

Along with full daily programs of activities and other onboard events, specialty lectures became an increasingly popular part of days in the 1970s and '80s onboard the likes of the *Canberra*. There were topics on history, beauty and fitness, films, architecture and even old ocean liners. Some of the most popular on ships such as the *Canberra* were also flower-arranging and floral design. And certainly, the most famous and popular 'florist at sea' then was Shropshire-based Howard Franklin.

Howard had his roots in shipping. 'Being a native of Liverpool, the greatest port in Britain, I was quickly intoxicated and fascinated by ships. As a child in the 1950s, I recall staring at the big Liver Building and Cunard headquarters, and fondly remember the school outings we had to ships in the port. While I would have liked to have been a farmer, I was trained as an art teacher and later in floral arrangement and design.'

Howard Franklin later became the most traveled floral lecturer on all the seven seas. By the late 1980s, he had done no less than seven world cruises and over 100 other voyages, many of them of the two- and three-week type. 'My sea-going career actually began with a phone call, almost out of the blue, in 1970 and from the P&O Lines in London. They had just decided to put a cultural lecture program on some of their liners. I was to offer one of three topics, with the others being bridge and art. Prior to that time, P&O had only port lecturers and ballroom dancing instruction.'

'My first cruise was a three-week trip in the *Oriana*, from Southampton to the Caribbean. There was lots of sea time and therefore lots of lecturing,' remembered Howard. 'Subsequent P&O trips followed onboard the *Arcadia*, *Orsova*, *Canberra* and *Sea Princess*. My favorite of all was the *Arcadia*, which had a very cozy, club-like atmosphere. She was a real ship in the old tradition and one onboard which you always felt welcome. My lectures tended to appeal to the more cultural passengers and often would draw as many as 400 and 500 per session.'

Howard later presented as many as sixty different lecture topics during three-month around-the-world cruises on the *Canberra*. His titles included:

Flowers & Shakespeare, Cooking with Flowers, Around the World with Flowers, Party Flowers, Flowers and the Theatre and *Abstract, Oriental & Modern Flowers.*

'Lectures are very important to cruises,' he added. 'Especially where there is lots of time at sea, passengers want mental stimulation. I have enjoyed bringing flowers onboard from different ports and then using them in my lectures. I have also led specialized shore excursions. A very special memory was to be greeted by Princess Grace at the Palace in Monaco. She had the best knowledge of flowers of anyone I'd ever met. Other visitations included the Los Quintos Gardens, owned by the Blandy family on Madeira. One of the most fabulous sites was on Majorca, owned by the exceptionally rich March family and which included a range from cacti from Arizona to English roses to South African proteas. There was, of course, tremendous advance planning for these visits. Just locating the garden of some obscure Spanish marquesa takes some effort.'

He also had some distinct preferences for his varied cruises on P&O. 'For botanic reasons, for pure superb natural geography, Capetown and Durban are two of my best favorites. Gastronomically, Palermo on Sicily has the best fettuccini anywhere. The finest sheer beauty of architecture might go to Naples, particularly the interior of the San Carlo Opera House. The most magical port is Santa Margherita, near Portofino in Italy. And the most spectacular arrivals and departures would be at New York followed by Sydney.'

Howard Franklin's first cruise on the *Canberra* was in January 1974. 'I was booked for the *Orsova*'s world cruise, but she was withdrawn and *Canberra* replaced her. *Canberra* actually adapted to an open-class ship better than any other P&O-Orient liners because of the flow of the public rooms. This was not, however, compromised by open class. Myself, I only traveled in first class accommodation with the fine dining in the Pacific Restaurant. Overall, the décor of the *Canberra* left much to be desired with a strong use of purple and orange, and horrific scarlet in the Meridian Room. Generally, the *Canberra* just could not compare to the *Oriana*, which was a classic Orient Line ship, not at all attractive from the outside, but truly a grand ship inside, especially with its Silver Grill on A Deck and restful interior colorings. Orient Line design was far superior to P&O. Orient Line was like staying in a stately country house whereas *Canberra* was like staying in a large, 1960s hotel. *Canberra* cruise passengers by the 1970s fell into two distinct groups. The old first class still attracted the aristocracy, captains of industry and the famous whereas the old tourist class was the Industrial North and the East End of London. The tourist class section and its passengers was the next best thing to a holiday camp!'

In all, Franklin did seven world cruises onboard the *Canberra*. 'The passengers were very loyal and returned year after year,' he noted. 'I especially recall Eleanor Hibbert [Jean Plaidy], the writer, who had her suite furniture rearranged to suit her needs. This involved the carpenters moving the desk and then, of course, bolting it to the deck in a different place. Eleanor became a dear friend and wrote the foreword to my first book on floral design. I recall many captains of the *Canberra* as well: Denis Scott-Masson, Ian Gibb and, of course, Fred Wolley, who was just the best ever. Pursers were mainly Alan Hale and Maurice Rudderham and Chief Engineer seemed to be always David Smith. I was the very first Special Interest Lecturer to be used. The rest of the team included Frank and Evelyn Jackson on ports, Nico Gardner on bridge, Margaret Newman on art, and Syd Perkin and Edna Duffield for dance. Indeed, they were happy days! Another thing I remember about the *Canberra* was the elegant social hostesses in their famous evening gowns. Roberta Pritchard, Tricia Trainor, Annette Bevan-Jones, Moira Wells, Shirley Golby and Christine Dorell, and all under the leadership of the best Cruise Director ever, Bill Allison.'

Dr Peter Crimes was another longtime, highly popular P&O lecturer. His specialty was port and regional histories and background. 'I have had a long association with P&O,' he recalled as we sat together some fifty-five years later on an Atlantic crossing aboard the *Queen Mary 2*. 'My family and I cruised on the *Chusan* in her maiden season, in 1950. It was a thirteen-day trip, from Southampton to Lisbon, Barcelona and Naples. It cost £36 per person or approximately $175 at the exchange rates of the time in an inside four-berth. The family lived like mice all year long and saved for one annual cruise. We tended to pick the then newer ships like the *Himalaya* and the mid-'50s "sensations", the *Arcadia* and *Iberia*. Once, however, we booked the old *Strathnaver* for a Baltic trip. But there were rumors of Second World War mines being still in Baltic waters and so the cruise was canceled and the trip on the *Strathnaver* dropped.'

Dr Crimes' first of his thirty trips on the *Canberra* was especially memorable. He became one of her port lecturers beginning in 1970. 'We took her shortly after her maiden voyage, in the summer of 1961, on a two-week Mediterranean cruise,' he recalled. 'She was absolutely revolutionary – a brilliantly designed ship. Except for the well-known 500 tons of concrete being in the bow section, she was the most revolutionary British liner in years. The cabins, for example, were much more modern, more spacious and actually quite plastic. Within, she had clean-looking décor and design. She had excellent upper, outer decks and very nice swimming pools. Even though she was two-class, even on cruises back then, you could still walk about almost everywhere onboard. The *Oriana* paled in design, I thought, by comparison. The *Canberra*'s restaurants were also innovative with alcoves and tables for two and four. But it was too dimly lit and so disappointed lots of little old ladies. Back then, P&O food even in tourist class was excellent. It started to decline in the 1970s as the Company cut costs and then the overall, onboard mood changed as well with the increasingly difficult British seamen's unions, world affairs and the rising cost of fuel oil. It was a sort of hit-and-miss with waiters and stewards. There were no comment cards then and so there was far less control. It was actually said to be far worse on the Orient Line ships, including the *Oriana*, where all-British crews ruled. P&O used Indian/Goanese staff that were, for the greater part, excellent. As recently as the 1950s, most Indian waiters could not read or write, but did it all by memory, serving three or four courses to eight and ten passengers. And it was all properly placed and paced as well. Their jobs were handed down from father to son and the fathers trained from a young age to work on ships, especially the big P&O ships. It was said that they had "brain training". The *Canberra* retained high-level Goanese always. The *Oriana* was less well run and even said to have more cockroaches!'

After Robert Pelletier moved from Massachusetts to southern Florida in the late 1970s, he headed a local ship enthusiasts' organization. 'I think the *Canberra* was the favorite ship of our local Steamship Historical Society Chapter,' he recalled. 'The highlight of our ship's tours was always the aft stairway with its memorial to her heroic work in the Falklands Campaign. After that, some of our members just enjoyed sitting in the Cricketer's Tavern.'

'*Canberra*, thoughtfully named after our capital, is a ship that plays a major role in Australia's small, but very enthusiastic, cruising history,' said Stanley Haviland, a Sydney-based passenger ship enthusiast and traveler. 'I visited her a number of times at Sydney and later, in 1994, did a six-day coastal trip on her. My earliest memories of her were of lots of linoleums and stairs. She always had this most amazing exterior, however, and the postcards of then up-and-coming Sydney in the '60s and '70s always seemed to show the *Canberra* at Circular Quay opposite the Opera House. She was usually on a "line voyage" from the UK, but by the '70s, she would avoid winter for two-three months of South Pacific cruising in our high summer. And sometimes, she operated in tandem with the *Oriana*. Both proved very successful and popular with Australians. The only difference seemed to be which you had first fallen in love with.'

'The *Canberra* was never based year-round in Australia, however, and unlike the *Oriana* that had her last five years of cruising based at Sydney,' added Haviland. 'But it was always exciting to know that the *Canberra* was in town and to know that there was nothing else quite like her in the world of ships. The *Oriana* was, I suppose, more evolutionary from earlier Orient Line ships and always filled me, to this day, with great passion. The *Canberra* was more

singular and a very proud ship. She had to be – she carried the name to the world of the capital of my beloved Australia.'

'To cruising Australians, the *Canberra* also represented a bit of glamour yet also a sense of coziness that made them feel at home, with bars such as the Alice Springs, where a good sing-a-long was part of a lunchtime glass of beer. People found their own levels of social standing onboard and it was interesting that the Purser's Lobby, which had been the division between the old first and tourist classes, still almost existed as a sort of imaginary line and until the very end of her days. Onboard comfort was often determined by cabin grades and this created a separation of sorts.'

In 1980, with fuel oil prices rising by the year, the *Canberra* was refitted at Southampton, given re-designed propellers and was fitted with new combustion material that meant she sailed slightly slower, burned less fuel and was generally more efficient.

There were some embarrassing moments in May 1981 when militant dockers at Southampton refused to handle the P&O flagship. Even though already docked, she had to depart and anchor off Spithead, offloading her 1,600 passengers and their luggage into ferries. Later, 1,400 outbound passengers and their baggage had to be ferried aboard from Portsmouth.

But almost worst of all, a BBC television crew went aboard the *Canberra* in 1981, supposedly to do a documentary on cruising. But instead of remaining in the passenger areas, the team went below decks and filmed a far different side of the beloved P&O flagship. 'They filmed crew drag shows, but then never mentioned in the final broadcast that it was in fact a crew show,' according to Dr Crimes. 'The ship and P&O itself were set-up. It was all about negatives. Millions of Britons saw the resulting footage on evening television and were horrified. The ship and her reputation were devastated. There was £500,000 in cruise cancellations in days.'

'She might have been finished, an unpopular and therefore uneconomic ship,' added Dr Crimes. 'But then there was the Falklands War, her heroic role and her return as a valiant ship. Instantly, she was again very popular and, it seemed, that all of Britain wanted to sail in her or sail again in her. Happy, profitable times were ahead.'

Above left: Nighttime at New York: *Canberra* was an addition to the New York waterfront during her 1973 cruise season. Like a chest of glittering jewels, she sparkled. (Fred Rodriguez Collection)

Above right: Overnight stay: dockside at Pier 86. (Fred Rodriguez Coillection)

Left: The vast, well-lighted upper decks. (Author's Collection)

Strung with festive lights. (Fred Rodriguez Collection)

The twin uptakes illuminated. (Fred Rodriguez Collection)

Evening departure for the sunny Caribbean, May 1973. (Fred Rodriguez Collection)

Other New York departures included daytime departures. She is seen taking on passengers at Pier 84. (Fred Rodriguez Collection)

Top: Throaty whistles signaled her farewell. (Fred Rodriguez Collection)

Above: A last glance as the ship enters New York's Upper Bay. (Fred Rodriguez Collection)

Left: Sharing the slip between Piers 84 and 86 with the Italian Line's *Michelangelo*. (Fred Rodriguez Collection)

Below left: Another departure but on a summer's evening in 1973. (Fred Rodriguez Collection)

Below right: A name known around the world. (Fred Rodriguez Collection)

Above: Early evening at New York, 5 September 1973. (Fred Rodriguez Collection)

Left: The mighty forward bow area. (Fred Rodriguez Collection)

Above left: Canberra in mid-Hudson, heading for Caribbean waters. (Fred Rodriguez Collection)

Above right: At anchor and tendering in the Caribbean. (P&O)

Left: Canberra visited ports of call around the world. Here we see her at Palma de Majorca. (P&O)

Above: Tendering in the Med. (P&O)

Above right: A festive departure. (P&O)

Below right: A favorite port: Sydney. (P&O)

Above: Passing at sea: The *Canberra* meets the *Iberia* in the Bay of Biscay. (P&O)

Above right: A call as Las Palmas in the Canaries. (P&O)

Below right: Sailing from Circular Quay at Sydney in a view dated February 1964. (P&O)

Above left: Dramatic setting: the *Canberra* by night at Sydney. (P&O)

Above right: Another nocturnal view at Sydney's Circular Quay. (P&O)

Left: Outbound at San Francisco and passing the famed Ferry Building. (P&O)

Opposite, above left: At Fort Lauderdale, Florida with the *Emerald Seas*, *Maasdam* and the *Crown Princess* in the background. (Port Everglades Authority)

Opposite, above right: At Lisbon and passing under that port's great bridge. (Luis Miguel Correia)

Opposite below: Outbound – in another view at Lisbon. (Luis Miguel Correia)

CANBERRA
LONDON

Two giants together – the *Oriana* (left) and *Canberra* together at Southampton on 3 September 1964. (P&O)

On 15 March 1966, on her first visit to Yokohama, the *Canberra* became the largest liner to visit Japan. Just ahead of her is another P&O liner, the *Chitral*, while the *George Anson* and the *Sagafjord* are berthed across the terminal. (P&O)

Three P&O–Orient liners in Southampton at the same time – the *Oronsay* (left), *Canberra* (middle) and the *Orcades* (right). (P&O)

Above left: At San Pedro, in the port of Los Angeles, the *Oronsay* passes the *Canberra*. (P&O)

Above right: The *Canberra* and *Sagafjord* as seen in a late afternoon view at Yokohama, on 15 March 1966. Both ships were on their maiden calls to that busy Japanese port. (P&O)

Right: The *Arcadia* (left) and *Canberra* meet in Sydney Harbor, 1966. (P&O)

Above: A less pleasant pairing of liners: the devastating British Seamen's Strike in the spring of 1966 crippled what was then the world's largest passenger ship fleet. In this aerial view at Southampton, among many others, seven ships are idle – the *Good Hope Castle*, *Reina Del Mar* and *Edinburgh Castle* are in the foreground, the *Arcadia* and *Canberra* are next, followed by the *S. A. Vaal* and the *Queen Elizabeth*, the largest liner in the world. (Southern Newspapers Ltd)

A stern view of the *Canberra* and *Arcadia*, which were nested side-by-side during the maritime strike of 1966. (P&O)

Seen here at Acapulco in 1972, the completion of the 17,300-ton, 742-passenger *Spirit of London* signaled P&O's deepening interest in the future of passenger shipping – in the leisure cruise trades. (P&O)

Opposite, above: In this occasion at Sydney, the *Oriana* is departing while the *Canberra* remains at Circular Quay. (P&O)

Opposite below: Rare occasion: *Canberra* departs from San Francisco with the *Oriana* still at berth. It was the only time the twin super-ships were at that California port at the same time. (P&O)

5

HEROIC DAYS: MISSION TO THE FALKLANDS

On a summer's evening in August 1982, I well recall sailing from Southampton. We were aboard the *Sea Princess*, bound for a two-week cruise of the Baltic capitals, which included the 27,000-ton ship's first return to Stockholm since her days as the Swedish American Line's *Kungsholm*. But, as we departed from the Western Docks, Berth 106, there were two sights of great interest. One was the *Queen Elizabeth 2*, sitting in the Ocean Dock and about to go off on a crossing to New York. She had just been refitted, following much publicized duties in the South Atlantic for the Falklands War. But the big notation was that she was rather suddenly repainted with a light gray rather than charcoal black hull. Like a woman not only in a new dress, but a different style of dress, the *QE2* appeared quite different. Myself, I was very surprised, in fact intrigued, by the new look for the Cunard flagship. The other, noted sight was of a liner, scarred in rust and looking very worn, also at the Western Docks. She was the *Canberra*, just home from Falklands duty and awaiting her refit for further commercial cruising. That evening, a Friday as I recall, she seemed especially lonesome, worn, tired, almost forgotten.

Earlier, Frank and Evelyn Jackson were onboard the *Canberra* in April 1982, as the liner was sailing westward in the Mediterranean, returning home to Southampton from her world cruise. 'We had 1,600 passengers aboard and a rumor started and spread quickly that we were going direct to the Falklands, which the Argentines had just invaded,' according to Frank Jackson as we cruised the Baltic together several years later in the summer of 1987, aboard the Mauritius-registered cruiseship *Astor*. 'But unexpectedly, the *Canberra* was ordered into Gibraltar Bay. Suddenly, British Army officers appeared onboard. Nothing was divulged, at least officially, until after our arrival at

Southampton, however. That same afternoon, a Monday and at 5:00 p.m., the *Canberra* was officially requisitioned. Everything not needed for the Falklands had to go ashore. Technically, she now belonged to the British Ministry of Defense. She had to be ready for war duty in three days! A big crane came alongside and lifted aboard a complete helicopter pad, for example. After leaving Southampton, she never touched port again for ninety-four days! My wife and I were along the Southampton Docks when she made her gala, triumphant return from the South Atlantic that July. There were whistles and horns blowing, flags and banners waving, bands playing and soldiers singing. It was a great day for a great ship that had a great record!'

The *Canberra*'s cruising popularity was actually sagging until her heroic work as a troopship in the Falklands War brought her renewed fame and a new generation of loyal and proud passengers. 'We were on the last part of the ship's annual world cruise. It was April 1982,' remembered Martin Reed. 'We were at Naples and there was a crew trip to the Vatican in Rome. I went along and presented Pope John Paul II with a *Canberra* mounted crest. The Goanese, mostly Catholic, were thrilled over the top! The next day, however, we received a signal from London to be prepared for something "extremely special", something "very unusual". It was all very hush-hush as we went directly to Gibraltar. The ship's future cruise program was suddenly uncertain. The next cruise was already cancelled. An advance party from the Ministry of Defense and P&O's London office joined us at Gibraltar and together began planning for the urgent transformation to transport at least 2,300 troops. Amazingly, the berthing plan was completed in one night! There were also plans for flight decks, which were already being prefabricated back in Southampton. Later, we had a very quick disembarkation of our 1,500 passengers at Southampton and then, within three days, shipyard crews built one flight deck and then a second. We sailed completely full for Freetown in West Africa and there disembarked the last of the work crews from the Vosper Shipyard at Southampton. They'd painted the flight decks with a mixture of paint and sand for a better stick for the aircraft. We then sailed to Ascension Island in the South Atlantic.'

The late Stanley Miller, an officer in the British-based World Ship Society, wrote to me in a letter dated 10 April 1982. 'Further to my last letter, the *Canberra* sailed last night at 8:00 p.m. from Berth 106 at Southampton with much cheering and on TV she looked lovely all lit up. One of the escorting tugs bore a sticker 'Good luck lads'. When the *Hermes* and *Invincible* sailed from Portsmouth, a popular song was sung with the words 'Kick the Bastards Out!' There were nearly 2,000 troops onboard with P&O staff plus the Entertainments Officer, who had volunteered to sail. Captain Scott-Masson was in command. All British merchant seamen taking part will get extra pay when in the danger zone below the Equator.'

'On TV, scenes onboard were shown,' continued Miller's letter. 'All troops have been ordered to wear soft shoes to protect the decks and carpets on the ship. All chandeliers and over 1,000 deckchairs have been put ashore. Officers are using the hairdressers' saloon as an office and we saw soldiers laying the tables in the former tourist class dining room. In the public rooms, sheets of hardboard are stretched through the middle to take the brunt of moving feet. Soldiers were delighted with their cabins they said. They were not amused, however, by the fact that fifty cases of Argentine corned beef had been taken aboard. It took two days for sheets of steel with steel supports to be placed over the midships swimming pool as a helicopter landing pad and also on the forward deck. Extra communication equipment has been taken aboard plus other sophisticated equipment. The *Canberra* has been fitted so she can be bunkered at sea from either RFA or chartered BP tankers. It is believed she will be based at Ascension Island. We will be getting daily TV reports from the joint BBC and ITV commentator onboard. All cruises up to 11 June have been canceled and consequently nearly 40,000 booked have been offered berths on later cruises or a discount on cruises on the *Sea Princess* or a full refund. In the travel world, there are rumors that the *QE2* may also be requisitioned.'

The *Canberra* was assigned to Ships Taken Up From Trade, coded STUFT, and was converted for trooping at Southampton in just three days. She stopped at Freetown en route to her South Atlantic duties and then, on 20 April, lay at anchor off Ascension Island. For days, she took on supplies, stores and fresh water. On 6 May, she joined a convoy headed for the troubled

Falklands. Within three days, with the Falklands under heavy attack, she became a 'dark ship' – all lights, even navigation lights, were extinguished at night. She was part of so-called Operation Sutton, the amphibious assault to reclaim the Islands. By 21 May, the *Canberra* was anchored off Fanning Island and soon afterward entered troubled San Carlos Water and, amidst continuous Argentine air attacks, began to embark her troops. So threatened here, two warships were lost to this war effort: HMS *Ardent* had been sunk and HMS *Argonaut* damaged. How the Argentine forces missed the big liner remains a mystery of the Falklands War. Fortunately, *Canberra* disembarked her 2,000 troops unharmed and headed for Grytviken on South Georgia Island to collect more troops. Further duties including trooping, taking on the sick and wounded, and carrying prisoners-of-war, which she delivered, under the guarantee of safety from the Argentine forces, to Puerto Madryn. It was, rather expectedly, a cool reception before the ship was back at sea. After further trooping and transport duties, she was ordered home, with 2,498 marines onboard, to the UK on 25 June. Five days later and out of Argentine military range, the blackout orders were canceled.

The British Government had promised that ships like the *Canberra* and also the *QE2* and another P&O vessel, the cruise ship *Uganda*, would not be at risk. 'But then we went into the battle zone in San Carlos Water and things were very close, very risky indeed,' added Captain Reed. 'The *Canberra* might have been hit, but the Argentines went first for the military escorts. The *Canberra* actually had three machine guns on each bridge wing and other machine guns aft of the funnels. There were continuous air attacks and threats. There were warnings all the time. It was also an exhausting time, but the P&O staff in particular were brilliant. There was a huge, pre-set process onboard: simultaneously feeding, sleeping and training our crew plus our military passengers. The troops, for example, wore sneakers very thoughtfully instead of boots so as to save the ship's teak decks. We had 130 tons of ammo on the open decks aft, a full hospital up and running in the Bonito Club and an operating theatre in the Stadium Lounge. The medics showed lots of training films, including rather graphic ones on 'sucking out' chest wounds. Even some big, tough Marines grew lightheaded and some even fainted. We handled three categories in the hospital: the "can't wait", the "near dying" and the "doomed". No wounded ever died on the *Canberra*, however, but some dead were brought aboard from other ships and later buried at sea. We returned to Southampton on 11 July, streaked in rust and weather-beaten, but to a huge, very joyous reception. The Prince of Wales came as well.'

The otherwise tired, rust-streaked *Canberra* had a triumphant return to Southampton on that warm summer Sunday in July. The 'Great White Whale,' as she was dubbed, came home to one of the most exciting receptions of any

British ship. Hundreds of small boats surrounded her, planes and helicopters flew overhead and an estimated 35,000 filled the docks and thousands of others lined the shore. In her ninety-four days as an urgent trooper, she had steamed 25,245 nautical miles, carried 6,500 troops and 4,200 prisoners-of-war. Her evaporators produced nearly 40,000 tons of water while her galley served some 650,000 meals. She was the most heroic British ship in years, since the dark days of the Second World War.

'I missed her sailing to the Falklands and also her return,' remembered David Hutchings. 'My first marriage at that time was reaching its final days, but I did watch a bit on television as she progressed in triumph on a green sea toward Southampton. A group of us drove past the docks as we headed to an engagement at Buckler's Hard in the New Forest that sunny day and saw a few remaining red balloons flying skywards and a mass of people, many of whom turned up in the Forest.'

Helicopters are stored on the reinforced upper decks. (Dr Rick Jolly)

Above left: The *Canberra* goes to war, south to the Falklands in May 1982. (Dr Rick Jolly)

Above right: Heroic ship: her return to Southampton from the South Atlantic on 11 July 1982. (Dr Rick Jolly)

Right: Hundreds of small boats escorted the battle-scarred ship, affectionately dubbed 'the Great White Whale'. (Author's Collection)

Within minutes, the *Canberra* will be berthed – her military duties over. (P&O)

Above left: Few ships have received a warmer welcome than the *Canberra* on her return from the South Atlantic. (P&O)

Left: The great ship approaches her berth – with thousands along the quayside. (P&O)

6

BACK IN BUSINESS

Myself, I was back aboard the *Canberra* as maritime lecturer for two cruises in the summer of 1983. She was still the beloved liner, but also the valiant, heroic ship. The Falklands War was still quite topical and the *Canberra* was a heroine of that South Atlantic conflict. Many recalled her triumphant return, mostly through the live, Sunday afternoon television broadcasts, of the ship to Southampton in July 1982.

'The *Canberra*'s role in the Falklands War was a huge success,' noted Dr Peter Crimes. 'On her first cruise after being refitted, in September 1982, she was escorted by Red Arrows overhead that gave off multi-colored smoke. War service resurrected her. Bookings climbed steadily and soon there were lots of full cruises. Lecturers were brought aboard to talk about the Falklands. It was widely believed that the *Canberra* went into conflict and therefore danger whereas the *Queen Elizabeth 2* did not go as far south or in as much danger.'

'A few visits onboard the *Canberra* whilst she was in Southampton were enjoyed,' recalled David Hutchings. 'I took a few low-quality interior shots and also I recall the event of the book launch of *Canberra – The Ship That Shaped the Future* by Neil McCart being held onboard. I was "hijacked" by a radio team to show them around and describe some public rooms. The event was also notable as I was introduced to Ken Vard who would later write his well-received *Liners in Art*.'

Jeffrey Willis managed the *Canberra*'s gift shops. 'By the 1980s and '90s, the *Canberra* was something of a British institution,' he said. 'She had loyal followers, some of them from day one. Even migrants who sailed her out to Australia returned. Yes, she had less amenities and public lavatories as

compared to a new generation of cruise ships, but she was popular, even beloved. In the end, she was like an old lady with great spirit. She was my first ship and so has a very special place in my heart. P&O was still very Royal Navy in ways. You would not even look at the captain, for example. But it was an idyllic experience – the ships, the ports, the people – and it all captured my spirit and imagination, and just like my Dad before in the Navy.'

Robert Pelletier recalls some press attention for the P&O flagship in January 1992. 'She was making what was to be her normal one day call at Port Everglades [Florida], but only to have a mechanical problem that required her to shift to a cargo pier for what turned out to be four or five days to affect repairs,' he recalled. 'Onboard, however, was a rather notorious British dominatrix whom Fleet Street newspapers had "outed" as having an affair with a Member of Parliament. The long layover gave the British tabloids plenty of time to have helicopters flying over the ship and badgering passengers and crew for any details about the lady in question, who was, of course, incommunicado aboard the whole time. With the Sheriff's Office as well as the ship's security controlling access to the gangway, I, as part of the port staff, could only issue a terse 'No Comment' as I would go to and from the ship. In retrospect, many unique passenger ships called at Port Everglades since the 1930s, but I think the *Canberra* was one of the truly unique and much loved ships to do so.'

But, of course, the cruise business is also very much about economics. Older ships and operating them were watched closely by Home Office accountants and then were featured items of discussion and evaluation in board room meetings. By the mid-1980s, for example, the *Canberra* was well into middle age for ocean liners. She turned twenty-five in 1986, in fact, and the same year that Cunard was refitting and re-engining the seventeen-year-old *Queen Elizabeth 2*. In fact, both the *QE2* and the *Canberra* were at the Lloyd Werft shipyard at Bremerhaven in northern Germany at the same time. The latter was in for her annual overhaul, but evidently there were some ideas being considered. 'There was a plan to convert the *Canberra* to more efficient diesels in 1985-86,' according to Captain Ed Squire. 'It would have meant that she would be completely rebuilt, the layout altered and her public rooms changed. Her engine room would have to be centralized, placed in a midships position. It would have given her an additional ten years' service, but the overall plan would have been too expensive and so P&O Cruises dropped the idea altogether.'

Within P&O itself, there were obvious, increasingly noticeable differences between the aging *Canberra* and, say, the new, 1984-built *Royal Princess*. About the same size at 44,000-tons, she was built in Finland for P&O's Princess Cruises division in North America. According to Captain Nick Carlton, 'Of course, the ships were designed and built for two different markets – an express, ferry-like liner and a floating resort for cruising. Fuel consumption was an increasingly worrisome component. The 22kt *Royal Princess* burned 70 tons a day [1986] whereas the *Canberra* burned 250 tons a day at 20kt and the twenty-six-year-old *Oriana*, then still based in Australia, burned 660 tons a day if pushed to 27½kt. Both the *Oriana* and *Canberra* were designed originally to sail at over 27kt. But by 1986, the *Canberra* had been fitted with new propellers for a more moderate 20kt. Ironically, the scrap value of the original phosphor-bronze props paid for the new bronze props. In the end, in 1986, her final P&O year, ships such as the *Oriana* were just not making enough profit. She had a mere 10 per cent return. There were rumors within the Company that she would be sold to the Greeks and so she was fondly dubbed the '*Orianis*' or that she would be sold to be rebuilt as a large Asian auto carrier. In fact, she was sold to Japanese interests, who brought her to a place called Beppu Bay for use as a moored hotel and museum ship. Later, however, she was sold to the Chinese and used by them at various ports including Shanghai until capsized in a typhoon in the port of Dalian in March 2004. She was later righted, salvaged but then scrapped in the fall of 2005. Operationally, the *Royal Princess* has bridge control whereas the *Canberra* still had telegraphs. And comparatively, there were forty-five engineers on the *Canberra* and five on the *Royal Princess*. It was all becoming more and more apparent and less so in the *Canberra*'s favor. She did, however, endure for another eleven years with P&O.'

Redecorating and restyling the 1980s and '90s. Here we seen the Crow's Nest in a view from January 1995. (Peter Knego Collection)

The Stadium Theater in a 1997 view. (Peter Knego Collection)

Above left: The upgraded Bonito Club. (Peter Knego Collection)

Above right: The Island Room. (Peter Knego Collection)

Right: The Century Bar. (Peter Knego Collection)

Another part of the Century Bar. (Peter Knego Collection)

The Ocean Room. (Peter Knego Collection)

The Meridian Room. (Peter Knego Collection)

The popular Cricketer's Tavern. (Peter Knego Collection)

Neptune's Lounge. (Peter Knego Collection)

A wing of the Neptune. (Peter Knego Collection)

The famous Spiral Staircase. (Peter Knego Collection)

Looking up along the Spiral Staircase. (Peter Knego Collection)

The Atlantic Restaurant as seen in 1992. (Peter Knego Collection)

The forward staircase. (Peter Knego Collection)

The Pacific Restaurant in a 1997 view. (Peter Knego Collection)

A mural on the forward staircase. (Peter Knego Collection)

An outside double on A Deck. (Peter Knego Collection)

The children's playroom. (Peter Knego Collection)

A B Deck double. (Peter Knego Collection)

Looking aft from the Bridge Deck in a view dated 17 March 1997. (Peter Knego Collection)

Above: Facing aft from the port-side wing. (Peter Knego Collection)

Below: A portion of the Sports Deck. (Peter Knego Collection)

Above: A night-time view of the upper decks from the Captain's Deck. (Peter Knego Collection)

Below: The aft pool. (Peter Knego Collection)

Along the port side of the Sun Deck. (Peter Knego Collection)

Above: A dramatic view from her bow. (Peter Knego Collection)

Right: Canberra's distinctive funnels. (Peter Knego Collection)

The wheelhouse. (Peter Knego Collection)

Above: The twin funnels. (Author's Collection)

Left: Always the beautiful, photogenic ship, the *Canberra* at Gibraltar on 14 October 1980. (Author's Collection)

The stern as seen during a visit to Tenerife. (Author's Collection)

Another view of the ship's funnels. (Author's Collection)

At Madeira, 18 October 1980. (Author's Collection)

Another view at Funchal, Madeira. (Author's Collection)

A poetic view at Funchal. (Author's Collection)

Above: Under the bridge – always an exciting moment! (Author's Collection)

Left: Passing under the harbor bridge at Lisbon. (Author's Collection)

The forward section as seen at Gibraltar. (Author's Collection)

Above: Also at Gibraltar. (Author's Collection)

Right: At sea, 1973. (Fred Rodriguez Collection)

During a Mediterranean cruise, 31 August 1981. (Author's Collection)

Anchored at Malta, September 1981. (Author's Collection)

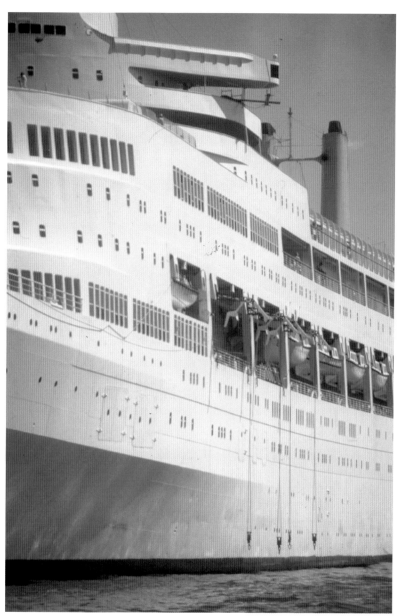

The towering port-side bridge wing. (Author's Collection)

Already twenty years of age by 1981, the *Canberra* was still an almost timelessly modern ship. (Author's Collection)

A leisurely late afternoon at sea, October 1980. (Author's Collection)

Another look at her distinctive twin uptakes. (Author's Collection)

Above: A quiet afternoon along the Sun Deck. (Author's Collection)

Top right: Shipboard leisure: conversations, a good book, a nap. (Author's Collection)

Right: More scenes of the *Canberra* from the early 1980s. (Author's Collection)

A quiet afternoon at Gibraltar.

Early morning in the sunny Med.

Farewell to Gibraltar, October 1980.

The quiet early morning.

Warm afternoon and bound for Naples, 1983.

Above: Fading sunlight off Portugal, 1980.

Right: The serenity of a warm afternoon in the Med.

With passengers still at breakfast, the *Canberra* heads for Cannes.

With her guests ashore, the great liner is berthed at Palma.

The top decks and funnels tower above the wharf.

Lazy afternoon near Malta.

Three liners at Madeira: the *Azur*, Chandris Cruises; the *Canberra*; and the *Cunard Princess*, Cunard. (Author's Collection)

Another grand meeting, but at Funchal, Madeira and in a view dated 22 April 1989 – the *Canberra* and the *Royal Princess*. (Luis Miguel Correia)

With their Falklands duties over, the refitted *Canberra* and the *Uganda* of BI Cruises are together at Southampton on 28 September 1982. (P&O)

First meeting: the inbound *Canberra* meets the brand new *Royal Princess* at Southampton in November 1984. The 44,000-ton *Royal Princess* became the new flagship of Princess Cruises. (P&O)

The two ships berthed at Southampton. (Southern Newspapers Ltd)

During their respective World Cruises, the *Canberra* (left) and the *Sea Princess* meet at Hong Kong. (P&O)

7

END OF A GRAND CAREER

P&O Cruises were competing more and more in the expanding British cruise market of the 1990s. Newer, flashier, better fitted and sometimes larger liners, indeed trim, well designed 'floating resorts', were coming in line. While beloved, still heroic and very popular, the *Canberra* was falling out of step. She was becoming costly, aged, less efficient, certainly less competitive. 'The onboard standards had improved by the early '90s,' according to Dr Peter Crimes. 'She was, however, still a very British ship – not an international cruise ship. The meals, for example, tended to revolve around roast beef and Yorkshire pudding, lamb and chicken. And there were still the curries at lunch.'

In 1995, P&O introduced their new *Oriana*, a 69,000-tonner built by Meyer Werft in Papenburg, Germany, with greater emphasis on creature comfortable amenities. Paired with the *Canberra* and despite some external similarity, the older ship had become more and more of a distant relative.

'Unfortunately, I was not in Sydney [in February 1997] to see the *Canberra's* last world cruise leave Sydney,' noted Stanley Haviland. 'I was in fact on the new *Oriana* and going the opposite way around the world. But I was thinking deeply of the emotions at Circular Quay. A friend, who loved the *Canberra* more than me, was aboard and so that was a consolation.'

But strange are the fates. Haviland was invited by shipboard lecturer Ken Vard to join *Canberra's* final cruise, a twenty-day voyage to the Mediterranean from Southampton, that September. 'Joining her at Southampton brought a whole new feeling for this aging dowager, still sparkling on the outside with layer upon layer of paint and yet the rust and decay eating her away well behind the scenes. I was lucky enough to have done the new *Oriana's* maiden

sailing and later the *Queen Mary 2's*, but the emotion of that farewell cruise and her final arrival from Southampton will never be forgotten or surpassed. I was on the monkey island above the bridge as parachutists with P&O flags and Union Jacks dropped from behind and as Canberra bombers and Air Force helicopters with red, white and blue smoke flew overhead. There were destroyer escorts and 10,000 colored P&O balloons were released from the netted swimming pools. There were thousands of people along the quayside and shorelines, and hundreds of small boats in Southampton Water. The *Last Post* was played as she arrived at 12 noon. The last return of that ship could not have been more emotional for me.'

Dr Peter Crimes recalled seeing the *Canberra* in her final days as well. 'I was aboard the *Victoria* in the summer of 1997 when we met the *Canberra* off Portugal. It was very nostalgic and sentimental. Still looking quite modern and certainly handsome, she sped past. These were the *Canberra's* last months,' noted Dr Crimes. 'Asbestos was, of course, the major problem in the end. Quite simply, it was too expensive to remove it. And then there were the economics. She was increasingly expensive to operate. She had that concrete in the fore end and this added drag and therefore more fuel was used. Also, she always had too much draft and so was limited in the ports that she could visit. But once the decision was made to withdraw her, there were long discussions in London on how to sell her. The question had two sides: for further service or for scrap. Lord Sterling himself favored the scrappers. He feared that loyalists would follow her to other owners.'

Jeffrey Willis was a shop manager who sailed on *Canberra* and made the last cruise. 'It was so sad. That last trip was booked two years ahead,' he remembered. 'She was a British institution and had loyal followers from day one and these included migrants. And even if she had less amenities, such as public instead of private lavatories in many cabins, she was, in the end, an old lady with great spirit. She had become heroic, of course, from the Falklands. She was a great ship. She had great character. She even had great curry. And she had some great characters in the crew and right to the very end. But when she went, they too vanished.'

Following the announcement months before that the *Canberra* was to be retired, David Hutchings was among many who was on alert for news of her final arrival in The Solent. 'This occurred on 30 September 1997 and so I joined one of the Gosport ferries, along with a young chum, Colin M. Baxter, then an up-and-coming watercolor painter, for a special excursion to welcome her home for the final time. But by the time we sailed, a thick fog had enveloped The Solent so our hearts sank as visibility – and our hopes of getting any decent pictures – fell to practically zero. Our vessel, however, sailed and we headed towards Calshot at the mouth to Southampton Water where our engines were almost stopped and we waited in the damp, gray gloom of that autumnal morning.'

'Then a few golden sparkles of sunshine highlighted the wavelets near to our craft and our spirits began to hope for a change in the weather,' added Hutchings. 'A Royal Navy frigate sailed by, inward bound amongst the crowd of waiting craft. Then, dramatically and ghost-like – almost in a replay of when I first saw the gorgeous *France* (but *sans* camera!) – the bow of the *Canberra*, a shade darker than the surrounding fog, appeared and soon to be followed by the rest of her magnificent bulk. Cameras clicked to capture the moment. From then on, the sun shone in increasing brightness as the old ship sailed towards her berth. Crowds on the ship hung various banners over her side and I, amongst hundreds of others, greeted her in return. I had taken my old Union flag that I had previously carried over the site of the *Titanic* the previous year. From then on, it was a grand, regal procession up Southampton Water. A festive occasion tinged in sadness. A Canberra jet flew overhead, sky divers fell to earth and streaming colored smoke behind them, and the first of many clouds of balloons arose from the great liner. A final berthing with some more excellent photographs being taken before it was time to return to Gosport.'

In their final years, just before their bankruptcy and then sudden closure in September 2000, Premier Cruise Lines had some ambitious plans, but none of which came to be. They wanted to supplement their existing fleet of secondhand cruise liners with further tonnage. They were going to buy, for example, the laid-up *Regent Sun* (ex-*Shalom, Hanseatic, Doric, Royal Odyssey*) and call her *Michelangelo*, using the artist's name in a pattern similar to the former *Rotterdam*, which became the *Rembrandt*. They also looked at buying the *Norway* (the former *France*), the Greek *Apollon* (ex-*Empress of Canada* and later the *Mardi Gras*) and the *Fair Princess* (the one-time Cunard *Carinthia* and ex-Sitmar *Fairsea*). But one deal actually came quite close. They were also going to buy the 44,000-ton *Canberra* from P&O. It was in the fall of 1997 and the 818ft liner was being retired by the British after thirty-six years of service.

Captain Nick Carlton was assigned to 'watch over' the ship during her final weeks and as she was being de-stored at the Southampton Docks. 'Negotiations were going on in our London office, but we were not always aware of the details,' he recalled. 'P&O was not, as it is often thought, averse to selling the *Canberra* for further cruise service with other owners just as long as she did not compete directly with them, say in UK cruising. That would be silly from a business point of view. But she could go, for example, elsewhere in the world, such as the Caribbean.'

Carlton had been aboard for her final cruise for P&O as well. 'It was a twenty-day trip from Southampton to the Mediterranean and there were lots of sentimentalists aboard,' he said. 'Afterward, I and a small crew stayed with her at the Southampton Docks. Premier Cruise Lines wanted to buy her, we were told, and sail her as the *Constable*. She was to be renamed for the English painter in the same way that the former *Rotterdam*, which they had just acquired, was renamed *Rembrandt*. There was also a Far Eastern buyer interested in the *Canberra*. But P&O had too many restrictions. They refused to allow any other owner to use the name *Canberra* or even mentioning it, or use the ship in any European service. They wanted $35 million for her, but then actually sold her for $5.6 million to an Indian scrap merchant, but for breaking-up in Pakistan. He was the same man who had bought another scrap-bound, P&O-owned ship, the *Fairstar,* formerly of Sitmar, and which he renamed *Ripa* for his daughter.'

'The *Canberra* was actually readied by P&O for further service with a new owner,' added Captain Carlton. 'P&O did take off some artwork such as the Maori canoe in the Pacific Restaurant, but maintained all the public areas and cabins as if she would continue sailing. It actually looked very promising that Premier would get her. But in the end, they could not come up with the money. And so, as we finished lunch one afternoon, a final decision was sent down from P&O headquarters up in London. She sailed that night with a P&O captain and forty-five crew onboard. She headed for the Med, then went through Suez, reached Karachi and finally arrived off Gadani Beach, also in Pakistan, where she would be beached, gradually hauled ashore and then broken-up. The whole process took a year and actually lost money for the scrappers. She was so solid, so heavy and so well built that the scrapping process was slow and difficult.'

David Hutchings remembered her final days at Southampton. 'A few weeks after her final arrival, the *Canberra* was transferred to the Queen Elizabeth II Terminal, a position that she had occupied during the naming of her new fleetmate, the *Oriana*, and that had taken place in the old Ocean Dock. It was rumored that the *Canberra* might be saved, perhaps by the Nation, and P&O did nothing to dispel these rumors as she was gradually de-stored. Finally, on her last day in Southampton, on 10 October 1997, by which time it was practically certain that her next stop would be the breaking beaches of India, I took the Southampton to Hythe ferry to take some last shots of her as she gleamed in the afternoon sun on an otherwise choppy, green, dockside sea.'

'That night, I was due to join a company skittles evening at Warsash on the River Hamble, just by its confluence with Southampton Water. About 9 o'clock, I said to my party that I was going out on to the beach to see if I could catch a glimpse of the old liner as she sailed by. A few joined me. The evening was cold with a keen wind. A moon illuminated a group of small clouds over Fawley on the opposite shore and where a few cars could be heard blowing their horns in a salute so I knew that the *Canberra* was approaching. An oil tanker at the Fawley refinery pier blew a farewell as she slid silently by, navigation lights burning but her decks in darkness. The moon shone down on her, reflecting on her white paintwork. A ghost, it seemed, was passing by in front of us.'

Keepsakes from bygone liners, especially famous and beloved ones such as the *Canberra*, are cherished and even more so these days. Captain Ed Squire was a fan of the P&O flagship and recalled, 'When the *Canberra* was being retired in the fall of 1997, most of her dining room china was sold to several restaurants in Southampton and surrounding area. Several years later, in April 2002, when I was sailing to New York on the *QE2*, I stopped in a Southampton restaurant called Michael's. I saw some of the *Canberra*'s dinner plates there, but failed to ask if I could purchase one. But when I boarded the *QE2*, I found a gift-wrapped package and birthday card waiting in my cabin. It was a beautiful piece of *Canberra* china given by my relatives from London.'

P&O Cruises added a succession of newer, larger, more extravagant liners following the retirement of the *Canberra*. In 2006, and along with the 1995-built *Oriana*, there is the 76,000-ton *Aurora*, the 44,000-ton *Artemis* (the former *Royal Princess* of Princess Cruises), the 77,000-ton *Oceana* (the former *Ocean Princess*, also from Princess Cruises) and the 82,000-ton *Arcadia* (at first intended to be the *Queen Victoria* for Cunard). There was also the affiliate *Ocean Village* for informal cruising and which had been the *Star Princess* and then the *Arcadia*. And on the order books for 2007 is the largest P&O liner ever, the 116,000-ton *Ventura*. Sold to Miami-based Carnival Corporation, which controlled a 49 per cent share of the entire world cruise market by 2005, the Company, still headquartered in London and still very British in style and tone, is in fact carrying more passengers than ever. British cruising is booming!

'Today, the British cruise market is buoyant,' according to Dr Peter Crimes. 'It has changed considerably as well. But perhaps the biggest change has been in entertainment. There was simply no planned or professional entertainment back in, say, the 1950s and aboard the likes of the old *Chusan* and *Arcadia*. There was a small band at each end of the ship, one for first class and the other for tourist, but otherwise the passengers themselves made the entertainment. Myself, I recall that on the first day after leaving the UK, passenger committee meetings were held. One was for entertainment and to plan shows. Another was for sports, for games and competitions. Everyone, even the very elderly, seemed to take part.'

'Back in the 1950s, cruising was the domain of an older clientele,' added Dr Crimes. 'But these days, everybody is going. There's all ages. P&O has grown from the days of the earlier, older liners in the '60s and '70s, and from their experiment with the budget ferry *Eagle*. For a time, the plan included cheap, cafeteria-style cruising to, say, the Caribbean. But instead, they looked to maintaining P&O and building on their great name. And sensibly in recent years, P&O has itself looked to a younger market. So along with P&O Cruises, there's Ocean Village and other innovations.'

P&O is great shipping history and their fleet long, distinctive, often noteworthy. But there was only one *Canberra*. She was unique, legendary, even a national institution as well as highly beloved and immensely popular. She deserves all accolades, praises and yet another biography. It is therefore my great pleasure to offer this tribute to a most splendid ship – the SS *Canberra*.

Once it was decided that *Canberra* would be retired, she made her final calls at many ports. Here she arrives at San Francisco for the last time in a view dated 14 March 1997. (Marvin Jensen)

End of a long and glorious career as *Canberra* arrives on her final cruise at Southampton in September 1997. (Clive Harvey)

Above: Balloons rise above the stern section as the ship arrives. (Clive Harvey)

Right: A sentimental last return. (Clive Harvey)

The great ship was lined with commemorative messages, many of them made by passengers and crew. (Clive Harvey)

Dressed in flags from end to end, the *Canberra* still looks a very modern ship despite her thirty-six years of service. (Clive Harvey)

Goodbye great lady! (Clive Harvey)

In a beautiful, but poignant painting, artist Robert Lloyd shows the *Canberra* being readied for scrapping at Gadani Beach in Pakistan.

Opposite, below left: A fireboat adds to the occasion. (Clive Harvey)

Opposite, below right: Today, P&O Cruises includes a modern fleet of cruise liners – including the 69,100-ton *Oriana* (seen here at Southmapton), the 76,000-ton *Aurora*, the 77,000-ton *Oceana*, the 44,000-ton *Artemis*, the 82,000-ton *Arcadia* and, due in 2007, the 116,000-ton *Ventura*. It is the larger and more popular than any time in P&O's 170-year history. (Peter Knego Collection)

BIBLIOGRAPHY

Braynard, Frank O. & Miller, William H. *Fifty Famous Liners, Volume I*. Cambridge, England: Patrick Stephens Limited, 1982.

Correia, Luis Miguel & Miller, William H. *SS Canberra of 1961*. Lisbon, Portugal: Liner Books, 1997.

Dawson, Philip. *British Superliners of the Sixties*. London, England: Conway Maritime Press, 1990.

Dawson, Philip. *Canberra: In the Wake of a Legend*. London, England, 1997.

McCart, Neil. *Canberra: The Great White Whale*. Cambridge, England: Patrick Stephens Limited, 1983.

Miller, William H. *British Ocean Liners: A Twilight Era 1960-85*. Wellingborough, England: Patrick Stephens Limited, 1986.

Miller, William H. *The Last Blue Water Liners*. London, England: Conway Maritime Press, 1986.

Morris, Charles F. *Origins, Orient and Oriana*. Brighton, England: Teredo Books Limited, 1980.